THE GOOD MORNING COOK BOOK

The Good Morning Cook Book

Jill M. Phillips

A FIREBIRD PRESS BOOK
GRETNA 2009

First edition, 1976
First paperback edition, 2009

Library of Congress Cataloging in Publication Data

Phillips, Jill M.
The good morning cook book.

Includes index.
1. Breakfasts. I. Title
TX733.P45 641.5'2 75-31702
ISBN-13: 9781589806931

Firebird, Firebird Press, a l are imprints of Firebird Press, Inc.
a division of Pelican Publishing Company, Inc.

Designed by Oscar Richard

Printed in the United States of America
Published by Firebird Press, Inc.
1000 Burmaster Street, Gretna, Louisiana 70053

Contents

To Mother and to Donna
Good cooks, good friends

Preface

Breakfast is probably the most neglected meal of the day, by cooks and hosts. Luncheons, on the other hand, are planned with delicacy, and dinners are prepared with the utmost care. Attitudes toward the morning meal do not change the fact that it is, according to doctors, the most important meal of the day. And most everyone agrees that a good breakfast is vital for an active day.

But isn't it unfortunate to think of breakfast as just another must in our lives? Americans are geared to pleasure, especially in their eating, and though there is pleasure in taste, food that is attractive and served with thought and order can make a smashing success out of what otherwise would be just another meal.

This book is intended to provide new ideas for breakfast preparations. Many of the recipes are geared to the host or hostess (or both) who is entertaining houseguests, and who wants to prepare a really nice morning meal. If you rely on this book, it is possible to create everything from the coffee, right down to the jelly spread.

Here are a few points to remember when you are planning a tasty and beautifully served breakfast for a number of houseguests or family members: first of all, do as much as possible the day or evening before. Breads, for example, which take a good bit of time to make, should be made well in advance of the meal. And though you cannot cook everything ahead of time, you can make a list of all the ingredients you will need for your various dishes, and you can set out many items for quick assembly and use. You can also set the table the night before.

Do inquire about preferences and things your guests can and cannot eat or drink. Tea or coffee? a choice of juices? Always have fruit juice on hand: pineapple, orange, grapefruit, apple, prune—all go well with any breakfast menu.

When serving pancakes or waffles, be sure that the syrup has been warmed. Nothing is quite so disappointing as cold syrup on nice hot cakes.

Try to balance your breakfasts with variety as much as you would for any other meal. For example, have something more than high-calorie sweets. Be prepared to serve a dish of baked eggs, rye toast, bran muffins, or fresh fruit.

If you are a jelly-jam-preserves maker, have lots of flavors available, and don't hesitate to offer a jar of something homemade to a guest. There is no warmer evidence of hospitality.

When you serve cold cereal, make sure that you have something hot to serve with it, if only a cup of Tomato Hot or steaming coffee or tea. Even on a summer day, don't serve all cold foods.

I hope that a great many men as well as women will enjoy these recipes when cooking for family and friends. Remember that cooking should be a happy experience and that breakfast is the day's first impression. Good luck!

PART I

Breakfast
Main Course Meals

Some breakfast items were meant to be served alone. When you want to serve a one-plate breakfast, try one of the following suggestions. They may take a bit of preparation, but they are all delicious and they look good too. Also, for a late breakfast, or even a picnic-style breakfast, these self-sustaining dishes are great.

Always remember that any of these recipes can be made with suitable substitutions and moderate variations—the Breakfast Pizza Leoni, for example. If you want to top the pizza with a few other favorites, feel free to do so. Or if you would prefer to cook the egg mixture before using it as a topping for the pizza, go ahead. In such a case, spread a small amount of butter over the eggs before putting the dish in the oven.

Also, these recipes, once made into serving reality, can be dressed up on the plate or platter with dried or fresh fruit slices. Any creative ideas you may have should be put into action.

BREAKFAST PORK CHOPS

3 tbsp. shortening
3 medium apples cut in 1/2-inch slices
12 thin pork chops
3 tbsp. butter
cinnamon-sugar for apples

Heat shortening in a large skillet or griddle. Add chops; keep heat at medium. Turn chops every so often until they are browned on both sides. Ten to fifteen minutes should be sufficient. Remove cores from apple slices; cook slices in butter in small pan over medium heat. Sprinkle apples with cinnamon-sugar. Remove chops to platter and top with apple slices. Makes 6 servings. These are great with scrambled eggs.

GLORIFIED FRANKS

6 link sausages
1 can sliced mushrooms
1/2 cup shredded cheese
1/6 tsp. pepper
6 hot-dog buns, split
8 eggs, beaten
1/4 tsp. salt
1/4 tsp. italian seasoning
butter or margarine

Fry sausages till well done; drain. Brown mushrooms in drippings using the same frying pan; drain. In another frying pan, combine eggs, cheese, mushrooms, and seasonings. Cook over low heat, stirring now and then until mixture is set but still moist. Toast buns and spread with butter. Spoon egg mixture onto buns and place a sausage in the center. Makes 6 sandwiches.

SCOTCH WOODCOCK TOAST

2 egg yolks
2 tbsp. light cream
1 small tube anchovy paste
2 slices hot toast, cut in halves
2 tbsp. butter
salt and pepper
1 tbsp. chopped parsley

Beat egg yolks in upper section of a double boiler until eggs are thick. Add butter, cream, and parsley. Cook over hot water, stirring till thick. Add salt and pepper to taste. Spread anchovy paste on hot toast. Pour egg mixture over toast and serve at once. Makes 2 to 4 servings.

HIDDEN SAUSAGES

1 lb. pork link sausages
1/2 tsp. salt
2 cups milk
2 cups sifted flour
4 eggs

Spread sausage links in a single layer in baking dish. Bake at 400° heat for 10 minutes. Meanwhile, combine flour, salt, eggs, and milk in bowl. Beat till smooth. Remove sausages from baking dish and measure 1/4 cup drippings—pouring off any remaining. Return measured drippings to baking dish, then pour batter into hot dish. Arrange the sausages on top of batter and bake at 400° for about 20 minutes. Reduce heat and bake for an additional 15 or so minutes. Let cool slightly before serving. This dish may be topped with jelly or jam. Should serve between 8 and 10.

BREAKFAST PIZZA LEONI

1 can biscuits
1/4 cup milk
1/2 cup grated cheddar cheese
butter
4 eggs
4 link sausages
pepper and salt

Brown sausages and drain on paper towel. Beat eggs in bowl; add milk and seasoning (pepper and salt). Melt butter in pan and add egg mixture; let cook over low heat for only a few minutes to allow eggs to cook only partially. Remove from heat. Now remove unbaked biscuits from can. Flatten each one to about the diameter of a grapefruit. Pinch edges up. Carefully spoon egg mixture onto each one. Slice sausages very thin and put equal amounts on each egg-covered pizza. Bake in preheated 400° oven for 8 minutes. Add grated cheese to top of pizza midway through baking time. Will serve 8 or 10 (depending on number of biscuits).

SAUSAGES IN BAKED BANANAS

6 bananas, unpeeled
6 medium-sized link sausages

Brown sausages in frying pan; drain and remove them to paper towel. Slit each banana lengthwise from tip to tip to form a pocket. Be careful not to cut through banana skin on the other side. Place one sausage in the opening in each banana. Arrange in baking dish, slit side up, and bake in moderate oven (375°) for 15 to 20 minutes.

HOT POTATOES AND BACON PLATTER

4 medium potatoes
6 strips bacon, diced (unfried)
1 tbsp. sugar
1/4 tsp. pepper
1/4 cup white wine vinegar
1/4 cup minced parsley
boiling salted water
2 tsp. flour
1/2 tsp. salt
1/2 cup water
1/2 cup diced onion
1/2 cup grated cheese

Cook potatoes in their jackets in boiling salted water to cover till done. Peel white hot and cut into slices. Fry the bacon till crisp and drain off all but 2 teaspoons of fat from the pan. Push bacon to one side of pan, sprinkle in flour, sugar, salt, and pepper. Stir till well mixed. Cook over low heat, stirring often for one or two minutes. Stir in bacon, vinegar, and water. Continue to cook till the mixture has thickened. Add potatoes, onion, and parsley. Heat thoroughly. Top with cheese and let melt a little. Mix. Serve hot. Makes 4 to 5 servings.

BANANA BREAKFAST SCALLOPS

1 egg
6 firm bananas, peeled
fat for frying
1/2 tsp. salt
3/4 cup cereal crumbs

Beat egg slightly and add salt. Slice peeled bananas crosswise into 1-inch-thick pieces. Dip into egg, roll in crumbs, and fry in deep hot fat (375°) for 2 minutes or until brown and tender. Drain and serve immediately. Serves 6. Bananas may be prepared for frying several hours in advance.

FRIED-EGG SANDWICHES

6 fried eggs
2 tbsp. butter
1 cup cooked tomatoes
dash of pepper
1/3 cup grated swiss cheese
1 small onion, minced
1 small green pepper, minced
1/4 tsp. salt
6 slices toast

Cook onion and green pepper in butter until tender. Add tomatoes, salt, and pepper and cook until reduced one-half. Spread sauce on fresh hot toast, place egg on each slice, and cover egg with grated cheese. Melt cheese by placing the sandwiches in broiler for about 1/2 minute. Serve hot with bacon curls. Makes 6 sandwiches.

BREAKFAST TREASURE CHEST

1 loaf unsliced bread
1/2 cup half and half
1/2 cup grated cheddar cheese
1 tsp. grated green pepper
butter
8 eggs, beaten
1/2 cup grated swiss cheese
1 tsp. grated onion
pepper and salt

Hull out the bread, leaving only a shell. Prepare egg mixture by combining eggs, milk, onion, green pepper, seasonings, and cheddar cheese. Melt butter in skillet and fry at low heat in pan. Butter inside of the hulled-out bread and place in 400° oven while cooking egg mixture in a frying pan. When mixture has set to the done point, take bread out of oven and spoon eggs into it. Cover with swiss cheese and pepper and salt. Return to oven and let bake for about 5 minutes (until cheese has melted). Will serve approximately 7.

SKILLET-STYLE BREAKFAST

1 large sausage (with skin)
5 medium-sized potatoes, pared and sliced
1/4 tsp. pepper
8 eggs
4 tbsp. butter
1 large onion, sliced
1/2 tsp. salt
2 tbsp. chopped parsley

Remove the skin from the sausage. Cut sausage into small slices. Melt butter in large skillet. Stir in the sausage, potatoes, onion, salt, and pepper. Cover. Cook over low heat, stirring frequently, until the potatoes are tender. Beat eggs in medium-sized bowl; stir in parsley; pour over the sausage mixture in the bowl. Cook over a low heat. Stir a few times while cooking (about 3 or 4 minutes). Eggs should set in that time. Spoon onto a serving platter. May also be served over scrambled eggs.

HAM-BANANA ROLL

6 thin slices ham
6 firm bananas, peeled
prepared mustard
cheese sauce

Spread slices with mustard. Wrap a banana in each ham slice and place in shallow baking dish. Pour the cheese sauce over bananas and bake for 30 minutes in a preheated oven at 350°.

MUSHROOM SCRAMBLED EGG SANDWICHES

8 eggs
1 cup mushroom soup
dash of pepper
16 slices buttered toast
1/2 tsp. salt

Beat eggs slightly. Add soup, salt, and pepper. Mix thoroughly. Pour into top of double boiler and cook over water till thick, stirring constantly. Spread between slices of buttered toast. Makes 8 sandwiches.

BREAKFAST BURGER

8 eggs, beaten
8 hamburger patties
1 tsp. diced green pepper
1 cup grated cheddar cheese
8 hamburger rolls
1/2 cup milk
1 tsp. diced onion
pepper and salt

In a frying pan, fry hamburger patties at medium heat. Heat oven to 400° and place the hamburger rolls (apart) on a cookie sheet. Let brown in oven for a few minutes, or until crispy. Meanwhile, mix eggs with onion, green pepper, milk, pepper, and salt in a mixing bowl. Melt butter in a skillet and pour in egg mixture. Let cook over low heat till eggs are done. Take the buns out of the oven and butter. Place hamburger patty on each one. Fill with eggs. Lettuce may be added, desired Serves 8

LEMON SOUP DISH

egg yolks
2 tbsp. flour
2 tbsp. butter
6 cups boiling water
peel of 1/2 lemon
juice of 2 lemons
1 tsp. vanilla extract
3 tbsp. confectioners' sugar

Melt butter and stir in flour. When well blended, add boiling water and lemon peel. Boil 5 minutes, taking care to keep it from settling on bottom of pan. In large bowl, whip egg yolks and sugar till thick and fluffy. Pour some of hot soup into bowl with eggs; beat well. Combine with rest of soup; reheat, but do not boil. Add lemon juice and vanilla extract and serve at once. Please, no crackers! Will serve 4.

FLORENTINE EGGS

2 boxes frozen creamed spinach
4 large tomatoes
salt and pepper
butter
8 eggs
1/3 cup shredded parmesan cheese

Butter a large flat baking dish or oven-proof platter. Spread cooked spinach evenly on dish. Sprinkle with 1/4 cup cheese and then poke eight holes in spinach with spoon. Break an egg into each hole, sprinkle with salt and remaining cheese. (Add 1 drop tobasco sauce if desired on each egg yolk.) Cut the tomatoes in half, place on another baking dish, and sprinkle with salt, pepper, and a pinch of butter for each half tomato. Put eggs and spinach in oven and place tomatoes under broiler. Bake eggs about 8 minutes. Serve with tomatoes. May also be served with sausages. Serves 8.

BREAKFAST CASSEROLE

1/2 box shredded wheat
1 can mushroom soup
1/4 cup chopped green pepper
butter
6 eggs, boiled, chopped
1/2 cup milk
pepper and salt
paprika

Blend together soup, milk, chopped boiled eggs, green pepper, and salt in a large mixing bowl. Add the shredded wheat. Place in a baking dish and bake in preheated 250° oven for about 20 minutes. Take out of oven and garnish with paprika and butter before serving. Will serve 5-6.

CHILLED CHERRY SOUP

1 can light sweet cherries
1 tbsp. sugar
1/4 cup frozen orange juice
dairy sour cream
nutmeg
1 can dark sweet cherries
1 lemon thinly sliced
1 1/2 tbsp. tapioca
dash of salt

Drain cherries, reserving syrup. Combine enough syrup to make 1 3/4 cups. Add orange juice (undiluted), tapioca, sugar, salt, and lemon together. Bring mixture to a boil in a saucepan for 10 minutes, stirring now and then. Cool and add cherries. Chill. Serve, garnished with sour cream and nutmeg. Makes 6 servings.

BREAKFAST SANDWICH TREAT

2 1/2 tbsp. butter
1/2 tsp. salt
1 cup shredded swiss cheese
1/4 cup grated parmesan cheese
1 can pineapple slices
2 tbsp. flour
1 1/2 cups milk
1/4 tsp. dill
4 english muffins
8 canadian bacon slices

Melt 2 tablespoons butter and stir in the flour and salt. Gradually add milk and cook. Stir often and cook till mixture thickens. Add cheeses and stir till they melt. Add dill. Set aside and keep warm. Melt the remaining butter in skillet. Drain the pineapple. Add to butter and cook till browned. Toast muffins. Remove pineapple from skillet. Add bacon to skillet and brown. Top each half of muffin with bacon slice. Spoon cheese sauce over each. Top with sautéed pineapple slice. Serves 8.

SCRAMBLED EGGS AND SAUSAGE CUPS

1 lb. pork sausage meat
1/2 tsp. salt
1/2 tsp. thyme
1 tbsp. butter
dash of pepper
1/2 cup uncooked oatmeal
1 egg
1/2 cup milk
1/3 cup milk

For the sausage cups, combine meat, oatmeal, 1/2 teaspoon salt, thyme, 1 egg, and 1/2 cup milk. Firmly press into custard cups. Place in shallow baking pan. Bake in 350° preheated oven for about 45 minutes. Unmold and drain on absorbent paper. For eggs, melt butter in a large frying pan over low heat. Beat together 9 eggs, salt, pepper, and 1/3 cup milk, till fluffy. Pour mixture into skillet. Cook till eggs have set. Arrange sausage cups around eggs on serving platter. Garnish with parsley. Makes 6 servings.

CURRIED GRAPEFRUIT

2 tbsp. butter
1/4 cup brown sugar
2 grapefruit, peeled, sectioned, and seeded
1 tbsp. curry
1/8 tsp. cumin

Melt butter, stir in sugar, curry powder, cumin. Add the grapefruit sections and simmer for 3 minutes, stirring gently and often. Makes 4 to 6 servings.

FRIED GREEN TOMATO SLICES

8 green tomatoes
pepper and salt
1/4 cup butter
chili powder (to taste)

Slice tomatoes in 1/2-inch slices. In a frying pan, melt butter at low heat. Fry tomato rings till nearly crispy; add pepper, salt, and chili powder. Serve hot. Serves approximately 8-10.

BACON OPEN-FACED SANDWICH DELIGHT

6 slices white bread
12 slices fried bacon
2 tbsp. butter
6 slices tomato

Butter slices of bread on both sides and place on pan. Fry till both sides are golden brown. Remove from skillet and top with 2 slices fried bacon. Place tomato slices (one each) atop toasted bread. Pepper and salt. Serve while bread is still hot from skillet. Serves 6.

PORK PATTIES IN A CHEESE SAUCE

1 lb. pork sausage
pepper and salt
1 can cheese soup
dried parsley

Heat skillet. Mold sausage into medium-sized patties. Place in skillet. Fry 5-7 minutes, or till done. Add cheese soup to skillet and continue cooking till pork is done. Soup will have the consistency of smooth gravy. Sprinkle parsley on patties and cheese. Serve pork, using cheese as a gravy. Serves approximately 8.

COTTAGE FRIED POTATOES

1 large pkg. hash brown potatoes
1 onion, diced
butter
1 green pepper, sliced
2 eggs, beaten
pepper and salt

Melt butter in skillet. In a mixing bowl, combine eggs, green pepper pieces, onion, potatoes, pepper, and salt. Mix thoroughly till well blended. Pour into skillet. Fry till golden brown, turning often with an egg turner. Serves approximately 6.

AVIATOR'S MIXED GRILL

Arrange this by supplying generous amounts of good link sausages, cooked pork sausages (grease drained), ham slices, bacon, and fish patties. Brush all with butter. Place, half cooked (except for pork sausages) over grill. Fruit juices and seasonings should be added, as well as butter. Cherries and oranges make a good complement too. Add pepper, salt, cinnamon, allspice, thyme, ginger, anything at all that strikes your fancy. And it certainly is.

PART II

Eggs and Omelets

Did you know that the middle-class citizens of ancient Rome ate eggs: And actually, they paid nearly what we do today for them. Although I don't know just how they fixed or served the eggs, the above fact does help to prove my point: eggs are breakfasts's most versatile ingredient.

Omelets, for instance. They can be fixed with nearly any type of filling. The ones I have included here are really just a tiny sampling of those that I felt were the most representative of what omelets can be. Also, if you, or those you are serving, happen to love cheese, then see fit to add a little shredded cheese to the egg mixture before you cook it, or before you fold the omelet. This can be done in the case of any type of omelet. It's pretty hard for cheese to offend a cheese-lover.

Just a hint on cooking omelets or scrambled eggs: Always make sure that the stove heat (or flame, if you cook with gas) is kept very low. Don't ever try to hurry eggs along by turning up the heat! Eggs set into hardness very quickly if they are not slowly cooked, and this not only makes them stiff and hard to work with, but unsightly as well.

CRANBERRY OMELET

4 eggs
4 tbsp. milk
3/4 cup premade cranberry sauce
1/2 tsp. salt
2 tbsp. butter

Directions for cranberry sauce

1 1/2 cups sugar
2 cups water
4 cups uncooked cranberries

Boil sugar and water together for 5 minutes. Add cranberries and boil without stirring until all the skins pop open. Usually 5 minutes is sufficient time. Then remove from the stove and allow sauce to cool in the pan. Yield will be approximately 5 cups of sauce. If you are making the 4-egg omelet (above) then be sure to store the remainder of sauce in the refrigerator. Even for smaller omelet, however, more sauce can be added than recipe calls for, if desired.

Directions for Omelet

Using the ingredients as written at top of page, prepare omelet thus: Beat eggs; mix thoroughly together with salt and milk. Melt butter in frying pan and tip to coat sides and bottom of the pan. Pour egg mixture into pan. Cook over a low heat, lifting the edges of egg mixture with a knife frequently so that the uncooked mixture will cook evenly. Loosen omelet from pan and spread with half the cranberry sauce. Pepper and salt may be used sparingly to spice omelet, but too much may spoil sweet taste. Remove from pan and serve on platter. Top with remaining cranberry sauce.

POTATO-STYLE OMELET

4 cold boiled potatoes
3 tbsp. bacon fat
1/2 tsp. salt
1/6 tsp. pepper
3 eggs
4 tbsp. milk

Cut potatoes into tiny pieces and cook them in the bacon fat with pepper and salt for about 5 minutes. Beat eggs in a mixing bowl and add milk. Pour mixture over the potatoes and cook till mixture has set. Fold omelet, then serve on a warm plate.

MUSHROOM OMELET

1 3/4 cups cooked tomatoes
3/4 cups sautéed mushrooms, thinly sliced
1 tsp. sugar
salt and pepper
4 medium-sized eggs
1/3 cup milk
1 tbsp. chopped onion

Add milk to eggs and beat well. In a frying pan, melt a little butter over low heat. Strain tomatoes, then add to sugar, onion, salt, and pepper in saucepan, cooking over low heat. Pour egg and milk mixture into frying pan. While omelet is cooking, pour part of the sauce over it before folding omelet. Fold, then place on plate. Pour remainder of the sauce around and on omelet and serve hot.

SPANISH OMELET

1 medium tomato
1 small green pepper
1/2 onion
2 sprigs parsley
olives
4 eggs
mushrooms
salt and pepper
1 stalk celery
butter

Peel tomato, then add pepper, onion, parsley, celery, olives, mushrooms, and cut together in a chopping bowl. Place mixture in a saucepan. Add seasonings and a dab of butter and cook for 2 to 3 minutes. Beat the eggs in a mixing bowl and put them, with a bit of butter, into an omelet pan. As soon as omelet begins to set, add vegetables. When omelet has set, fold and serve on a warm plate.

FANCY OYSTER OMELET

1 small can oysters
1/3 tbsp. flour
2 tbsp. fat
2/3 cup light cream
4 eggs
salt and pepper

Chop oysters finely. Make a sauce of the flour, fat, and cream. Add well-beaten eggs, season with salt and pepper, then stir in oysters. Place mixture (with small amount of melted butter) into frying pan at low heat. When mixture has stiffened sufficiently, fold omelet, and then serve on a warm plate.

RASPBERRY-STYLE OMELET SOUFFLÉ

1 (10 oz.) package raspberries
dash of salt
2 tbsp. butter
2 tsp. lemon juice
4 eggs, separated
1/2 cup sugar
confectioners' sugar

Thaw the raspberries and sprinkle lightly with the lemon juice. Then beat egg whites with salt until foamy. Slowly beat in the sugar until mixture is stiff and glossy. Beat egg yolks lightly. Fold yolks into egg whites.

Melt butter in an oven-type skillet pan and heat to bubbling. Pour the egg mixture into pan and bake at 375° for 10 minutes or until golden. Remove from oven and slide onto warm serving plate.

Slit omelet at top, down the center. Cut to bottom. Spoon half the berries into slit. Spoon remaining berries onto top of omelet soufflé. Sprinkle top with confectioners' sugar. Serves 6.

CHEESE-BACON OMELET

4 strips unfried bacon
1/4 cup grated cheddar cheese
pepper and salt
4 eggs
1 tbsp. butter
3 tbsp. milk

Fry bacon; drain and lay aside. Beat eggs, add milk, salt, and pepper. Melt butter in another frying pan and add egg mixture. While omelet is cooking, cut bacon into small bits. Add cheese and bacon to top of omelet, fold, then serve. Garnish with more pepper and salt.

COUNTRY (VIRGINIA) OMELET

1 cooked potato, thinly sliced
1/2 cup cooked ham, diced
salt and pepper
1 onion, sliced
1/4 cup butter
4 eggs, beaten
butter

Sauté potato and onion in hot butter in a skillet till well cooked. Stir in ham and quickly cook till crisp. In another pan, melt butter and add well-beaten eggs. As mixture begins to thicken, add ham, onion, and potato. Place omelet pan under broiler; broil, watching closely until it is well done and brown on top. Serve warm, on hot plates. Garnish with parsley, if desired.

FRENCH CHEESE OMELET

4 eggs
6 tbsp. milk
1/8 tsp. salt
1/2 small pkg. processed cheese thinly sliced
dash of pepper
1/8 tsp. dry mustard
2 tbsp. butter

Beat eggs until whites and yolks are well blended. Add salt, mustard, pepper, and milk; mix well. Heat butter in skillet (moderately hot) till melted. Pour egg mixture into skillet. Cook over a low heat. As egg mixture cooks around edges, lift gently with spatula so as to loosen. When mixture is firm throughout, cover entire surface of omelet with thinly sliced cheese. Cook until cheese begins to melt and bottom of omelet is firm. Loosen sides with spatula; fold in half. Turn out on a hot platter or plate. Serve at once.

APPLE OMELET

4 eggs
2/3 cup applesauce
butter
4 tbsp. milk
pepper and salt

Prepare omelet by beating eggs together with milk and adding pepper and salt. Melt butter in a skillet, and keep over low heat. Add egg mixture. Cook until omelet is firm, loosening sides with a spatula. Cover one-half of omelet with applesauce; fold over and remove from pan to hot platter. Serve at once.

SCRAMBLED EGGS PLUS

8 eggs
1/2 cup diced cooked ham
1/4 cup diced pimento-stuffed green olives
1/2 tsp. salt
1/2 cup grated cheese
butter
pepper

In a mixing bowl beat eggs, salt, and pepper just enough to combine egg whites and yolks. Add ham, cheese, and olives; stir well. In a large skillet, heat one or two tablespoons butter. Add egg mixture. Cook gently, stirring occasionally until eggs are set as much as desired. Then serve at once. Makes 4 to 6 servings.

BAKED NEST EGGS

2 pkgs. frozen mixed vegetables
2 tbsp. butter
6 smoked link sausages (small size)
1/4 cup milk
6 eggs
3 english muffins, cut and toasted
paprika

Combine frozen vegetables with milk and butter and heat, following label directions. Stir in sausages, after first slicing each one crosswise. Spoon into a greased, shallow 6-cup baking dish.

Break eggs, one at a time, into a cup, pouring each into vegetable mixture, spacing evenly. Sprinkle with paprika. Bake in 400° oven for 20 minutes, or until eggs are set and vegetables bubble up. Place each muffin-half on heated serving plate; lift eggs and vegetables with pancake turner or slotted spoon and then place on muffins. Serves 6.

SCOTCH EGG ROLLS

6 hard-cooked eggs
2 eggs, beaten
deep fat, enough for frying
1 1/2 lbs. sausage meat
cracker meal
pepper and salt

Peel eggs, then dip into beaten egg mixture. Wrap each egg in a thick coat of sausage meat. Dip again in egg. Roll in cracker meal. Add pepper and salt. Fry in deep fat (as with french fries) for 5 minutes. Drain and let cool slightly. Serves 6.

EGGS-IN-A-BUN

6 eggs
1/6 tsp. pepper
2 tbsp. butter
1 1/3 cup grated cheddar cheese
1/2 tsp. salt
1/4 cup minced green pepper
6 hot-dog buns, toasted

Beat eggs, salt, and pepper with a fork or beater. Add green pepper. Heat butter in a skillet until hot enough to sizzle a drop of water. Pour in the egg mixture and then top with cheese. As mixture thickens, lift from bottom and sides with spatula to let thin uncooked part of mixture flow to bottom. However, avoid constant stirring. Cook until eggs are thickened but still moist. Spoon onto the toasted buns. Makes 6 servings.

AVOCADO-EGG SCRAMBLE

3 avocados
8 eggs
3/4 tsp. salt
2 tbsp. chopped onion
6 slices fried bacon, cut into pieces
lemon juice
1/2 cup milk
2 tbsp. butter
pepper
few drops hot pepper sauce

Cut avocados lengthwise into halves. Remove seeds and the skins. Coat with lemon juice. Beat eggs into milk, add salt, pepper, and hot pepper sauce. Melt butter, add onion, in frying pan. Cook lightly. Add egg mixture and cook over medium-low heat stirring occasionally, until eggs are almost set. Spoon over avocados. Garnish with bacon pieces. Serves 6.

MUSHROOMED SCRAMBLED EGGS

8 eggs, slightly beaten
2 tbsp. butter
parsley
1 can mushroom soup
pepper and salt

Stir soup until smooth; blend in eggs, pepper, and salt. In a skillet, melt butter; pour in egg mixture. Cook over low heat, stirring occasionally till eggs have set. Serve at once. Makes approximately 6 servings.

SCRAMBLED EGGS IN BOLOGNA CUPS

8 eggs
1/4 cup grated cheese
6 slices bologna
parsley
2 tbsp. milk
pepper and salt
2 tbsp. butter
paprika

In a mixing dish, beat eggs with a fork until smooth; add milk, pepper and salt. In one frying pan, heat a tablespoon of butter till melted and hot. (Do not overlap bologna slices; you may have to do them in batches.) The slices will slowly puff in the middle. Meanwhile, heat 1 tablespoon of butter in another frying pan and pour in egg mixture. Add half of cheese. Let cook until set. When bologna slices have inverted, put onto plate and fill with cooked eggs. Top with cheese; garnish with parsley and paprika. Serves 6.

CHEESE BAKED EGGS

2 cups milk
salt and pepper
1/6 tsp. hot pepper sauce
10 eggs
1 cup shredded cheddar cheese

Beat together milk and eggs. Season with pepper, salt, and hot pepper sauce. Sprinkle cheese into greased baking dish. Carefully pour in egg mixture. Bake at 350° for 45 minutes to 1 hour. Makes 8 servings.

SCRAMBLED EGGS WITH BACON AND CORN

10 eggs
1/3 tsp. salt
pepper to taste
12 slices bacon, fried
1 can cream-style corn
grease from fried bacon

Beat eggs with fork until mixture is smooth. Add salt and pepper. Heat bacon grease in skillet. Add the egg mixture, and stir in corn. As eggs are beginning to set, crumble bacon into small pieces and add to the pan. Stir eggs until done. Remove from pan. Sprinkle with parsley if desired. Serves 6.

BREAKFAST EGGS WITH RICE
(Special Chinese Tea Eggs)

8 eggs
3 tbsp. black tea
2 cups cooked brown rice
water
1 tbsp. salt
1 cup melted cheese

Place eggs in water to cover and bring to a boil over medium heat, then cook gently for 10 to 12 minutes. Reserve the water. Cool eggs thoroughly under cold running water for 5 minutes. Roll each egg gently on a board or table to crackle the entire shell. (Do not remove the shell, however.) Bring reserved water to a boil once more. (There should be 3 to 4 cups; if not, add more water.) Add tea, salt, and crackled eggs. Simmer, covered, until egg shells turn brown; about 45 minutes. Turn off heat and let eggs stand, covered, for about 30 minutes. Drain eggs, cool and shell. In a saucepan blend cooked rice and melted cheese. Heat over low flame or heat for a few minutes. Add salt. Slice eggs in half and dish rice-cheese mixture over them. Serves approximately 6.

HERBED BREAKFAST EGGS

6 hard-cooked eggs
1 tsp. lemon juice
2 tbsp. butter, melted
1 tsp. mixed salad herbs
1/4 tsp. cayenne pepper
1 tsp. dry mustard
2 tsp. mayonnaise
pepper and salt
minced parsley
paprika

Shell hard-cooked eggs, cut in half (lengthwise), and remove the yolk. Mash yolks mixed with lemon juice. Add mustard, mayonnaise, butter, herbs, salt and pepper, cayenne pepper, and mix well. Pile filling into egg white and garnish each with a sprinkle of parsley, and paprika. Makes 12 halves. Will serve 6, allowing 2 halves for each person.

EGGS, WESTERN STYLE

10 eggs
1 small jar minced dried beef
1/2 cup milk
pepper and salt
1 bag frozen french fries
1/2 cup shredded cheese
parsley
lard

In a large frying pan, melt lard at medium heat. In a mixing bowl, mix eggs and milk together, until creamy. Add cheese, pepper, salt, beef. Set aside and cook the french fries in a pan with melted lard. Turn to high heat. Use an egg turner to mash fries until they have the consistency of hash brown potatoes. Add egg mixture when the potatoes are brown. Cook mixture at low heat until eggs begin to set. Stir occasionally. When eggs are done, remove from pan and garnish with parsley. Serves 6 to 8.

CUBAN-STYLE EGGS

8 eggs
1/2 cup sausage meat
1 tbsp. chopped onion
1/2 tsp. salt
pepper
paprika

Cook sausage and onion together for 5 minutes. Beat eggs in mixing bowl until smooth, add seasonings, and pour into pan with the meat. Cook slowly, stirring constantly, until mixture is thick and creamy. Serve with buttered toast. Garnish with paprika. Will serve 6 to 8.

ELEGANT BAKED EGGS

6 eggs
1/2 cup grated swiss cheese
1 tbsp. chopped onion
1 medium-sized can crushed pineapple, well-drained
2 cups cooked rice
1/2 cup dairy sour cream
1 tsp. chopped parsley
liquid red pepper spice
pepper and salt

Combine drained pineapple with rice, sour cream, cheese, onion, parsley, salt, pepper, and liquid red pepper spice. Spoon into 6 individual buttered baking cups. Press rice against sides of cups, leaving a depression in the center. Bake in moderate 350° oven for 15 minutes. Break and drop an egg into each depression, bake 10 minutes longer. Serves 6.

SCRAMBLED EGGS WITH LETTUCE

8 eggs
1/3 cup fine-curd cottage cheese
2 tbsp. butter
1/2 cup finely chopped lettuce
pepper and salt

Melt butter in frying pan. In mixing bowl, beat eggs till smooth. Add salt and pepper. Pour eggs into pan. When set, add lettuce and cottage cheese. Serves 6.

FLUFFY CHEESE EGGS

6 slices toast
6 eggs
1 cup grated sharp cheddar cheese
butter
1/2 tsp. salt
12 strips bacon, fried
pepper and salt
paprika

Spread toast with butter and part of grated cheese. Separate eggs (put egg whites into mixing bowl, leave yolks in shell) season egg whites and beat with fork until mixture is stiff. Heap onto toast and make a dent in the center of each. Slip yolk into center of white, season and sprinkle with cheese. Bake in moderate (350°) oven till cheese is browned and eggs have set through. Top with two bacon strips each and garnish with paprika. Serves 6.

BAKED EGGS ESPAGNOLE

6 eggs
3 tbsp. chopped onion
3 tbsp. chopped green pepper
pepper and salt
4 tbsp. fat
1/4 cup bread crumbs
1/2 cup grated cheese
paprika

Fry onion with salt and pepper in the fat until onions are slightly brown. Pour into greased baking dish. Break eggs into the dish, being careful not to break yolks. Mix bread crumbs with cheese and sprinkle over eggs. Bake in a slow oven (250°) until eggs have set. Garnish with green pepper, salt, pepper, and paprika. Serves 6.

EGGS à la SUISSE

6 eggs
2 tbsp. butter
1 cup grated swiss cheese
1 cup heavy cream
salt and pepper
paprika

Spread butter over the bottom of a baking dish. Sprinkle a layer of cheese over it. Break eggs on the cheese, careful not to break yolks. Pour cream over eggs, then add more cheese. Season with pepper, salt, and paprika. Bake in preheated 350° oven for approximately 15 to 20 minutes. Makes 6 servings.

FRIED SEASONED EGGS

6 eggs
pepper and salt
2 tbsp. butter
1 tbsp. thyme

Melt butter in frying pan over low heat. Break each egg into pan, being careful not to break yolks. Add pepper and salt. Before turning eggs, sprinkle with thyme. Turn eggs and sprinkle other side with thyme. Remove from pan and serve. Serves 6.

ONION FRIED EGGS

6 eggs
2 tbsp. chopped onion
2 tbsp. butter
pepper and salt

Melt butter in frying pan; add onion. Cook over low (very low) heat for approximately 10 minutes, or till onion is tender. Remove onions from pan. Break eggs into pan being careful not to break yolks. Cook to turning point, then cook other side. Add pepper and salt. Garnish with cooked onion. Serves 6.

PART III

Pancakes and Waffles

It seems that there are two types of people in the world: those who love pancakes, and those who don't like them at all. Therefore, if you are serving a large group—and have within that group some who do and some who don't—try this: Prepare the pancake mixture the night before, and store in the refrigerator. That way, while you are busy preparing another type of breakfast for the nonpancake lovers, you will at least be spared the time of mixing the pancakes. Actually, if timed properly, they don't take a great deal of time to fry; it's the mixing that takes the much-needed time in the morning. If you do this, you will probably want to add a little milk or water to the mixture that will no doubt have become a bit thick overnight.

The Turkey Breakfast Pancakes can be served as a sort of special type morning or late morning meal. The inspiration for this particular dish will most likely have been a turkey dinner the night before. This is a fine way to serve breakfast and really good, nutritious food at the same time, as well as a weapon for warding off early-dinner appetites.

OLD WEST SOURDOUGH PANCAKES

(If you do not have a cup of the Starter for this kind of recipe, it is easy enough to make your own, provided that you start two days ahead of the time when the pancakes will be needed.)

For starter

1 pkg. yeast
2 cups sifted flour
2 cups warm water

For pancakes

2 cups starter
2 cups sifted flour
3 tsp. baking powder
1 tsp. soda
2 eggs, beaten
1 cup milk
1/4 cup sugar
1 tsp. salt
1/4 cup oil

Directions for starter

Combine ingredients in a large mixing bowl; mix well until satisfactorily blended. Let mixture stand uncovered in a warm place (80° to 85°) for 48 hours. Stir it a few times. To use, stir and pour off as much as the recipe requires. Replenish the remaining starter by adding equal parts flour and water to the mixture. Stir and let stand a few hours until it bubbles again, before covering loosely and refrigerating. The starter should be replenished about every two weeks.

Directions for pancakes

Beat together starter, milk, and flour until all are well blended into a smooth mixture. Let it stand in loosely covered bowl in a warm place for at least 12 hours. Add remaining ingredients and stir till smooth. Bake on a lightly greased preheated griddle, or in a frying pan, using one tablespoon of batter for each pancake.

PEAR AND SWEET POTATO PANCAKES CALIFORNIA STYLE

3 California pears
2 cups grated raw sweet potato
1 tbsp. flour
1 tsp. salt
1 cup sugar (fine white)
1/4 cup evaporated milk
2 eggs
dairy sour cream
grated orange peel
brown sugar, to taste

Core, halve, and cut the pears into small and even wedges. Chop part of the pears to make 1 cup and cover remaining pear wedges to serve as a garnish for the pancakes.

Combine the grated sweet potato with flour and milk. Beat eggs into mixture one at a time and add the salt. Mix in chopped pears. Drop by spoonfuls into well-greased frying pan or onto well-greased griddle. Cook the cakes slowly—giving them approximately 10 minutes on either side, turning only once.

These pancakes can be served with a variety of toppings, but here we have included the following: remainder of pear slices, one spoonful (per cake) sour cream, brown sugar and orange peel. These are not only delicious, but they look pretty too. Serves 6.

MARCO POLO WAFFLES

2 cups milk
2 squares unsweetened chocolate, melted, cooled
2 eggs
2 cups prepared pancake mix
1/3 cup melted shortening
pinch of nutmeg

Place milk, eggs, and shortening in a medium-sized but deep bowl. If melted shortening is used rather than liquid shortening, add after pancake mix. Add the pancake mix, and then add the chocolate. Beat the mixture with a rotary beater, until the batter is smooth and creamy. Bake in hot waffle iron until done through.

When serving, top the waffles with Banana Jam (see recipe in this book) which is a marvelous compliment to this breakfast delight. However, other spreads, or fruit jams and jellies can make nice additions to this dish. Will serve 6.

LE GRAND ORANGE-STYLE PETITES

1 small box pancake mix
3 tbsp. softened butter
1 egg
1/3 cup confectioners' sugar
1/2 cup orange juice
milk
grated rind of 1 orange
1 tsp. cooking oil

Mix pancakes according to recipe on box, adding milk, eggs, and cooking oil with pancake flour in a large mixing bowl. Then, in a separate bowl, mix butter, sugar, and orange together. Melt butter in a skillet and fry pancakes. Set to cool. Spread orange mixture on cooled pancakes, roll up, and put back into the skillet. Add orange juice and heat till juice bubbles. Serve at once. Makes 12 petites (2 for each, if serving 6 people).

SOUR CREAM-COTTAGE CHEESE PANCAKES

2 eggs
1/3 cup cottage cheese
1/2 cup sifted flour
1/2 tsp. salt
3/4 cup sour cream
1/2 tsp. soda

Since these pancakes have the old fashioned flavor, it is best to mix them slowly by hand, so that the mixture will remain thick and a bit lumpy. Now sift the flour, soda, and salt together. Put the eggs into a bowl, and beat them gently with a fork until well mixed. Add cottage cheese and stir. Add sour cream and mix till thoroughly blended; about 3 minutes. Add flour slowly and stir. Let mixture stand for about 10 minutes. Then fry on a moderately hot griddle. If pan is too hot, outer sides of pancakes will cook quickly, but the thick inner mixture will not. Serves 6 to 8.

MONOGRAM PANCAKES

3 cups pancake mix
1 cup milk
1/4 cup sugar
1 large egg
1 cup water
1/4 tsp. salt

Blend ingredients together carefully, making sure that the mixture is smooth when mixed. Heat griddle to high heat. Before the pancakes are poured onto griddle, use a spoon to pour on desired initial letter. Brown lightly, then turn initial to brown on other side. Pour pancake batter for one pancake over each initial made. This will make approximately 6 to 8 pancakes and their initials. Especially nice for children.

APPLEJACKS

6 eggs
1 1/2 tsp. salt
melted butter or margarine
1 can presweetened apple pie filling
1 1/2 cups sifted flour
1 1/2 cups milk
1 small can applesauce

Beat eggs slightly, then beat in flour, salt, and milk. Continue to beat till mixture is smooth; then let stand at room temperature for 30 minutes. Then add the apple pie filling. Heat griddle and fry cakes at medium temperature. Turn each cake only once. When cakes are done, serve at once with a small amount of butter and top with canned applesauce rather than syrup. Serves approximately 6.

OATMEAL-BUTTERMILK PANCAKES

1 cup uncooked oatmeal
2 tbsp. sugar
2 cups buttermilk
2 cups pancake mix
1 tbsp. salad oil
1 egg

Mix pancake batter according to the box instructions, blending liquid ingredients slowly, carefully. Then blend in the oatmeal. Heat the griddle to a medium, rather than high heat. Carefully pour ingredients onto griddle and fry cakes. Mixture will be thick and therefore pancakes will be thick. Turn only once. Makes approximately 8 to 10 pancakes. Serve with butter and apple butter.

PANCAKES a ' la SAUSAGE

1 lb. sausage roll
1 cup pancake mix
1 tbsp. salad oil or melted butter
1 1/2 cups buttermilk
1 egg

Slice sausage into 20 thin slices. Mix the other ingredients to form the batter. Then brown sausage slices on both sides (lightly) in a large-sized skillet. When this has been done, drain patties on paper napkins or towels to remove the grease. Pour 20 pancakes onto hot griddle, placing a sausage patty in the center of each. Fry pancakes till done, turning only once. Top with honey, jam, or syrup. Makes 20 pancakes.

FRENCH CAKES WITH JELLY

3 cups pancake mix
3 tbsp. sugar
2 cups milk
1 egg

Mixture here will be thinner than ordinary pancakes. Blend ingredients together according to box instructions. Then let mixture sit for about 30 minutes. This will allow time for mixture to thicken a little. Make cakes larger than most. Keep griddle at medium heat. Serves 6 to 8 people. Top with fruit jelly or fresh fruit, along with butter—and love.

BREAD CRUMB GRIDDLE CAKES

1 1/2 cups dry bread crumbs
1 1/2 cups scalded milk
1 tbsp. shortening
1 egg, beaten
1/2 cup sifted flour
1/2 tbsp. salt
3 tbsp. baking powder

(Depending on taste, either add sugar to taste, or pepper and salt to taste. In other words, if "sweet" cakes are what you're looking for, add sugar to the mixture; if spicy, bread-type cakes are desired, add pepper and salt.)

Soften dry bread crumbs in milk and shortening. Add egg and dry ingredients, mixed and sifted. Bake on a hot and well-greased griddle. The cakes should be turned carefully, since they are tender and crumble easily. This batch should yield 10 to 12 pancakes.

CORNMEAL WAFFLES

1 1/2 cups boiling water
1 cup cornmeal
1 tsp. salt
4 tbsp. shortening
2 eggs, separated
1 cup sifted flour
1/2 tsp. baking soda
2 tsp. baking powder
1/2 cup milk
2/3 cup buttermilk

Add boiling water to cornmeal and stir in salt and shortening. Cook in a double boiler for approximately 10 minutes, with only occasional need for stirring. Then let stand to cool. Add beaten egg yolks. Sift flour with soda and baking powder and add alternately with the milk. Now add enough buttermilk to make a pour batter. Fold the stiffly beaten egg whites into the batter. Bake in a hot waffle iron. Will make 6 waffles. Serve butter and peach jam or Fruited Syrups (see recipe in this book).

TURKEY BREAKFAST PANCAKES

For filling

1 cup chopped turkey
1 can cream of celery soup
2 tbsp. buttermilk pancake mix
1/4 tsp. salt
1/2 cup grated sharp cheddar cheese
1/4 cup chopped onion
1/2 cup chopped celery
1/8 tsp. pepper
2 tsp. lemon juice
1/4 cup chopped pimento
10 pancakes
2 cups milk

Keep pancakes warm between paper towels or in a pan in the oven. Then remove pancakes from oven and heat oven to 400°. Mix turkey, onion, half of cheese, celery, pimento, and lemon juice together in mixing bowl. Spoon two tablespoons of mixture onto each pancake. Roll pancakes into cone shape. Put folded side down in 1" x 7" baking dish. Heat in the oven for approximately 10 minutes. Mix soup, pancake mix (two tablespoons), salt, pepper, and milk together in saucepan and heat till thickened. Pour over rolled-up turkey pancake cones and sprinkle with remaining cheese. Place cones under broiler heat for a very short time—until cheese is bubbly. Serves 10. Perfect for a making-an-impression-on-the-company meal.

CREAM WAFFLES

2 cups sifted flour
1 tbsp. cornmeal
1 tsp. baking soda
1/2 tsp. salt
2 eggs, separated
2 cups sour cream

Sift flour, cornmeal, soda, and salt together in a mixing bowl. Then beat egg yolks and add cream. Mix in the sifted ingredients; mix well. Set aside. Use rotary beater to mix egg whites, till stiffly peaked and firm. Blend into other ingredients. Bake in a hot waffle iron. Will make 6 waffles. These are delicious when served with strawberry jam.

CRANBERRY CAKES

3 cups pancake mix
1 egg
1 cup tart cranberries (cooked and softened)
1/2 cup sugar
2 cups water

Mix pancakes according to instruction, adding egg, water, and sugar carefully. Heat griddle to medium heat; keep well greased. Add cranberries to mixture.

APRICOT-NUT FLUFFY PANCAKE CONES

For filling

1 small pkg. cream cheese, softened
1 small can unpeeled apricot halves (drained)
1/4 cup slivered almonds

For pancakes

3 cups complete pancake mix
1/2 cup sugar
1 2/3 cups water

For filling, beat the cream cheese until it is fluffy, then add the apricot halves. Stir in the almonds and let the mixture sit at room temperature while preparing pancake mixture. Now, for pancakes, place dry pancake mix, sugar, and water into deep bowl. Stir lightly until batter is fairly smooth. For each pancake, pour approximately 1/6 cup batter onto hot, lightly greased pan or griddle. Turn only once. After removing pancakes from the pan, spoon mixture in between each cake and then roll into cone-shaped cakes. Serve while hot, and top with butter, and apricot jam, if desired. Makes approximately 6 cone-shaped cakes.

CHEESE WAFFLES

1 cup sifted flour
1 egg
3/4 cup milk
1/2 cup cubed cheddar cheese
1 tbsp. sugar
1 tsp. baking powder
2 tbsp. melted butter

Use blender to mix milk, egg, butter, sugar. When blended, add cheese, and mix thoroughly. Add flour and baking powder. Cook in hot griddle iron. Makes 3 to 4 waffles.

PART IV

Breakfast Salad Bowls and Fruits

Here is the ideal breakfast for the calorie conscious or weight watcher. These treats can be made even more so by the substitution of certain low-calorie ingredients, although most of these are sure beltline watchers in themselves. None of them are difficult to prepare, and they offer the one creating them a certain amount of freedom because, really, the possibilities are legion. There is no reason in the world that a salad can't be served as successfully for breakfast as it is for lunch or dinner. Salads are certainly healthful and pretty to look at, and they can be used to improve any menu.

As mentioned above, the person who must watch calories can help the salads along by substituting for some of the higher calorie ingredients—such as sugar, for example. Use honey instead. Let these salad ideas be used to augment your own vivid serving imagination, and then create your own variations from these guidelines. Your guests or family will be more than pleased, and you will be proud.

Hint: Never make salads too far in advance of the meal (jello molds would be the exception here), and don't (unless the recipe here states otherwise) make them the night before. Salads that use tomatoes, lettuce, or other fresh fruits and vegetables may wilt if they sit too long in the refrigerator. None of these salad bowls take a great deal of time to make, so be sure to make them in the morning—for the sake of freshness.

SUMMER COMPOTE

3 plums
1 cup orange juice
2 bananas
3 nectarines
1/2 lb. grapes (purple)

Peel nectarines. Slice pulp off the plums. Combine in a jar. Peel and slice bananas. Add to nectarines. Also add grapes. Pour in orange juice to barely cover. Cover jar tightly and refrigerate overnight. Spoon into fruit dishes putting some of each fruit into each dish. Makes 7 servings.

HONEY-LACED GRAPEFRUIT

3 large grapefruits, sliced in half
1/2 cup honey
2 tbsp. red cinnamon candies

With a sharp knife, cut around each grapefruit to loosen from membrane. Remove seeds. With scissors, cut out center core and membrane from each grapefruit half. Combine honey and cinnamon candies in a small saucepan. Stir over low heat until candies dissolve. Spoon honey mixture over grapefruit halves and broil for 3 minutes or until top of grapefruit is bubbly. Makes 6 servings.

POACHED ORANGES

6 oranges
3 tbsp. butter
1 tbsp. potato starch
1/2 cup orange juice
3/4 cup currant jelly
2 tbsp. cold water

Remove thin outer rind from three of the oranges and cut into thin slivers. Place rind in a small pan with water. Cover; bring to boil. Reduce the heat; simmer for 10 minutes. Drain, reserving rind. Cut the remaining peel and white from all oranges. Place large crepe pan or skillet over canned heat flame. Add butter and jelly and stir till melted. Stir in orange juice and slivered rind. Add oranges and cook gently, spooning sauce over oranges, for about 5 minutes. Mix together potato starch and water to form a smooth paste. Stir into sauce in crepe pan. Continue to stir over heat till thickened. Continue the spooning of sauce over oranges till heated through. Serve warm, covering oranges with sauce and slivered rind.

MORNING TOMATO SALAD

- 1/2 cup mayonnaise
- 1 tsp. minced onion
- 1/4 tsp. salt
- 6 hard-cooked eggs, chopped
- 3/4 cup diced cooked ham
- 1 tsp. prepared mustard
- white pepper to taste
- 4 large tomatoes
- 1/2 cup diced celery

In a medium-sized mixing bowl, thoroughly stir together mayonnaise, mustard, onion, salt, and pepper. Add eggs, ham, and celery—toss lightly. Remove stem end from the tomatoes. Cut each tomato down almost to bottom to make six wedges. Pile egg salad on each tomato. Place on a lettuce leaf. Makes 4 large servings.

PEARS SUZANNE

- 10 canned pear halves
- 10 tbsp. red tart jelly
- cinnamon-sugar
- butter

Place pear halves on cookie sheet. Place in preheated 400° oven for about 7-9 minutes. Midway through cooking, sprinkle with cinnamon-sugar and butter. When pears have cooked, spoon jelly into the center of each. Serves 5.

FRESH FRUIT CUP BREAKFAST

- 3 small apples
- 1 grapefruit
- 1 large orange
- juice of 1 lime
- 2/3 cup cherries
- 1/2 cup strawberries
- 3 peaches
- 1 cluster purple grapes
- watermelon slices
- 1 banana
- juice of 1 lemon
- 1/3 cup blackberries

Cut between 25 and 30 small watermelon pieces from the slices; chill in refrigerator. Peel apples; slice into small pieces and place in large bowl. Remove pulp from grapefruit and orange. Separate sections. Wash cherries, grapes, and put them with sections in bowl. Peel and slice banana. Add to all other fruit. Pour juices of lime and lemon over fruit. Stir lightly. Chill for 1/2 hour before serving. Will serve 5.

MORNING MINT PLUMS

1 pkg. cream cheese
1 tbsp. grated lemon peel
2 tbsp. powdered sugar
6 fresh mint sprigs
1 tbsp. lemon juice
6 fresh California plums

Combine cream cheese with lemon peel and juice. Mix in a little powdered sugar. Cut a large wedge from each plum and fill cavity with mixture. Garnish with a little sprig of fresh mint. Chill briefly before putting on the breakfast table. Serves approximately 3.

BAKED APPLES IN ORANGE SAUCE

8 small baking apples
1/2 cup flour
2/3 cup sugar
1/2 cup orange juice
1/2 cup butter
1/2 tsp. cinnamon
1/4 cup water

Pare and core apples. Arrange in a buttered baking dish. Combine flour, sugar, butter, and cinnamon. Mix together. Fill cavities of apples with cinnamon crumb mixture. Sprinkle remaining crumbs over top of apples. Add water and orange juice. Bake in moderate (375°) oven for about 45 minutes. Will serve 8.

CRANBERRY AMBROSIA

2 cups sugar
3 cups water
2 cups uncooked cranberries
2 apples
2 oranges

Boil sugar and water together for 5 minutes. Add peeled and sliced apples; cook slowly for 15 minutes. Add oranges (cut in thin slices) and cranberries; continue cooking for 10 minutes. Serve in small glass bowls. Will serve approximately 4.

APPLE-RAISIN MORNING PLATE

2 cups diced, unpeeled apples
1/2 cup raisins
1 cup chopped nut meats
1 cup diced celery
1/3 cup mayonnaise

Mix the ingredients, tossing lightly so as not to harm or bruise the fruit. Chill in the refrigerator for 1/2 hour before serving. Will serve about 4.

DANDELION BREAKFAST SALAD

1 cup watercress
1 1/2 cup dandelion greens
6 thin slices raw onion
lemon juice

The dandelions should be fresh and young and unmarred. Wash leaves carefully and drain well. Arrange in a salad bowl (glass is best) and add watercress. Add slices of onion and then drizzle lemon juice over salad. Chill in refrigerator before serving. Will serve 3.

BANANA-NUT EYE-OPENER

4 bananas
1 cup chopped nuts
1/2 cup mayonnaise
6 lettuce leaves

Peel the bananas. Cut in two (lengthwise). Roll each half in nut meats. Place on individual lettuce leaf and garnish with mayonnaise. Will serve 6.

EARLY-MORNING JELLO MOLD

1 pkg. lemon gelatin (already made)
1 cup plain yogurt
6 slices fresh lemon

The jello can be made the evening before. In the morning, spread the yogurt over the top of gelatin. Garnish with lemon slices. Will serve 5.

DESERT BREAKFAST PLATE

1 cup figs
1 cup raisins
1/2 cup chopped nuts
lettuce leaves
1 cup dates
3 bananas, diced
1/3 cup plain yogurt

Combine all ingredients except lettuce and mix carefully. Chill in the refrigerator for about 1/2 hour, before serving. To serve, place on individual lettuce leaves. Will serve 6.

GRILLED GRAPEFRUIT WITH SPICE

3 grapefruit, sliced in half
whole cherries
cinnamon-sugar mixture

Preheat oven to broil. Sprinkle grapefruit halves with cinnamon-sugar and place under broiler for about 4 minutes. When cooked, place a cherry on top of each half; fasten with a toothpick. Will serve 6.

BROILED BANANAS IN SAUCE

6 bananas, peeled
2/3 cup pineapple juice
1 cup crushed cornflakes
nutmeg

Heat oven to broil. Roll bananas in fruit juice, then in the cornflake mixture. Sprinkle with nutmeg. Place under the broiler for about 3 minutes, till cornflake topping is browned and banana is cooked through. Will serve 6.

HOT FRUIT BOWL

1 can fruit cocktail (small size)
cinnamon

Drain most of the juice off the cocktail. Place in a saucepan and heat to boiling point. Add the cinnamon before serving in small soup bowls. Will serve 3 to 4.

GRAPEFRUIT AND GRAPE SALAD

2 cups grapefruit sections
1 tbsp. white wine
2 cups white grapes

Peel large grapefruit and separate the sections. Be sure to remove every bit of bitter white membrane from the grapefruit. Peel and seed the grapes and mix with grapefruit sections. Drizzle the wine over fruit. Chill in the refrigerator for about 1/2 hour before serving. Will serve approximately 4.

HULA BOWL

2 cups drained crushed pineapple
3 bananas, peeled, sliced
2/3 cup flaked coconut
1/2 cup chopped nuts
3 tbsp. pineapple yogurt

Mix all ingredients together in a salad bowl. Chill in refrigerator before serving for about 1/2 hour. Will serve approximately 4.

TOMATO BASKETS

6 medium-sized tomatoes
2/3 cup sliced green pepper
cottage cheese
paprika

Cut tops off tomatoes and remove insides. Fill each tomato with cottage cheese. Sprinkle with diced green pepper and garnish with a small amount of paprika. Will serve 6.

FRUIT STEW

1 cup dried prunes
1 cup dried apples
1 cup raisins
4 cups water
1 cup dried apricots
1 cup dried figs
1 cup dried peaches

Place all ingredients in a large pan with the water. Cover and steam at low heat for about 30 minutes, or until fruit is very soft. Serve hot. Will serve 5-6.

STRAWBERRY YOGURT BOWL

2 boxes frozen strawberries
1/2 cup confectioners' sugar
3 cups plain yogurt
mint sprigs

Wash, hull, and drain strawberries. Slice about a cupful of the berries and place in a bowl. Sprinkle with several tablespoons of sugar. Let stand for half an hour or so at room temperature, then fold in yogurt and mix. Pour yogurt sauce over them. Sprinkle with more sugar, and garnish with mint sprigs. Will serve 6.

MORNING GRAPEFRUIT SALAD

grapefruit halves
dairy sour cream
romaine lettuce
mint sprigs

With a sharp knife, remove sections from shell of grapefruit. Cut membrane away from sections. Place the romaine inside of grapefruit shells, and pile sections on top of that. Pour thinned sour cream over sections and top with a mint sprig.

FLORIDA BREAKFAST PLATE

4 red apples
2 oranges
cottage cheese
2 bananas
1/2 cup raspberries
leaf lettuce

Remove peels from oranges and bananas. Wash raspberries and place in a large salad bowl. Slice oranges and bananas into small, but not tiny, pieces. Pare and core apples, slice into small pieces, and add to the bowl mixture. Fold in a liberal amount of cottage cheese and toss gently. Place lettuce leaves on individual plates and top with salad. Will serve 4.

PART V

Rolls, Muffins, and Breads

Perhaps nothing so cheers or perks up a breakfast table as warm rolls and muffins from the oven, or a slice of sweet fruit bread. Naturally, these can be served alone, as a solo breakfast menu, or they can be well complemented by eggs, sausages, bacon, or a warm beverage.

Here again, the possibilities are great. Practically any type of fruit can be used for breads and muffins and just about any type sauce will go well with the rolls.

All breads included here, however, are not of the sweet type. Carrot Bread, for example, and the Brown Bread offered here in this book, are fine examples of the more severe type of recipe standby. If served as the only item on the breakfast menu, they are good indeed with a small amount of cream cheese used as a spread.

Muffins, like breads, seem to grow even tastier when they are stored in waxed paper or foil for a while, say for a few days. However, biscuits or rolls made for breakfast should be served for that meal and not allowed to sit till the next meal, or the next breakfast.

If you are looking for something really exotic to use as a spread for the Cheese Bread, try a light paste, anchovy, for example. Or even use small-curd cottage cheese.

Corn bread, of course, is best served with butter. Scones (a fine, if offbeat breakfast addition, originally Scottish) can be served the same way, or topped with one of your homemade jellies or spreads (which will be detailed a little later in this book). Or try sour cream.

APPLE-DATE-NUT LOAVES

- 2 1/2 cups sifted flour
- 1/4 tsp. ground nutmeg
- 2 tsp. baking powder
- 1/2 cup butter
- 1 cup milk
- 3/4 cup chopped walnuts
- 1 cup chopped, peeled, cored apples
- 1 tsp. baking soda
- 3/4 tsp. cinnamon
- 1 tsp. salt
- 1 cup sugar
- 1 egg
- 1 cup chopped, pitted dates

Heat oven to 350°. Grease loaf pans with unsalted shortening and coat with flour. In a bowl, sift together flour, baking powder, baking soda, cinnamon, nutmeg, and salt. In a large bowl, mix butter and sugar well. Add egg to the butter mixture and beat till blended. Add flour mixture alternately with milk to butter mixture and blend well. Stir apples, dates, and walnuts into batter. Pour batter into pans. Bake for approximately 60-65 minutes. When breads are done, remove from the oven and let cool for about half an hour, or even a bit longer. When cooled, the loaves should be wrapped in foil or waxed paper and stored in the refrigerator overnight. Also, when served, bread should be sliced very thin.

DATE-NUT BREAD

- 1 cup boiling water
- 3/4 cup chopped pitted dates
- 1/4 tsp. ground cinnamon
- 1 tsp. baking soda
- 1/4 cup shortening
- 3/4 cup firmly packed brown sugar
- 1/4 cup orange juice
- 1 1/2 cups sifted flour
- 1/8 tsp. ground mace
- 1/2 tsp. salt
- 1 egg
- 1 cup chopped pecans
- grated orange rind

Mix boiling water, orange juice, and dates in a large mixing bowl and let stand at room temperature. Heat oven to 325°. Grease loaf pan and coat with flour. Sift together flour, cinnamon, mace, baking soda, and salt. In a large bowl mix shortening and brown sugar till blended. Add egg to the shortening mixture and beat till blended. Stir date mixture, beating till blended, then stir into shortening mixture. Add dry ingredients to batter and mix till moistened. Fold nuts and orange peel into batter. Pour batter into pan and bake for 65-70 minutes, or till done. Makes one loaf.

CARROT BREAD

4 eggs
2 tsp. baking powder
1/2 cup oil (shortening)
2 cups finely grated raw carrots
2 cups sugar
3 cups unsifted flour
1/4 tsp. salt
2 tsp. cinnamon
1 1/2 tsp. baking soda

Preheat the oven to 350°. Beat the eggs, then add sugar; beat till thick. Add oil. Stir in flour, baking powder, salt, soda, cinnamon. Stir in carrots till well blended. Pour into greased loaf pans. Bake for 1 hour. Makes 2 loaves.

PRUNE BREAD

2 cups sifted flour
1/2 tsp. salt
1 tsp. soda
1 egg, beaten
1/4 cup shortening
1/2 cup chopped nuts
1 tsp. baking powder
1 cup finely chopped prunes
1 cup boiling water
1 cup sugar
1 tsp. vanilla

Line the bottom of a loaf pan with waxed paper. Sift flour, baking powder, and salt together in a large mixing bowl. Combine prunes, soda, and boiling water. Add the shortening, sugar, and eggs. Mix thoroughly. Add nuts and vanilla. Add dry sifted ingredients and stir well. Turn into loaf pan and let stand for half an hour. Bake in preheated 350° oven for one hour.

CHERRY BREAKFAST BISCUITS

1 can dark pitted sweet cherries
3 cups biscuit mix
1 1/2 tsp. grated lemon peel
1/2 cup sugar
1/4 cup butter
1 cup cottage cheese
1/2 cup milk

Drain cherries, cut into halves. Combine biscuit mix, 1/4 cup sugar, and 1/2 teaspoon grated lemon peel. Cut in butter. Stir in milk to form stiff dough. Roll out to a long rectangle. Combine cottage cheese, sugar, and 1 teaspoon lemon peel. Spread mixture over dough. Sprinkle with well-drained cherries. Roll up, beginning at wide end. Cut into 12 slices. Place on greased baking sheet and bake in preheated 375° oven for about 30 minutes. Serve warm. Will make 12 biscuits.

BACON MUFFINS

- 2 cups sifted flour
- 2 tbsp. sugar
- 1/2 cup grated cheese
- 4 slices bacon, fried crisp and crumbled
- 3 tsp. baking powder
- 1/2 tsp. salt
- 1 egg, slightly beaten
- 2 tbsp. oil
- 1 cup milk

Sift flour, sugar, baking powder, and salt together into a bowl; stir in cheese and bacon. Mix egg, milk, and oil in a smaller bowl; add them to flour mixture. Stir with fork till evenly mixed. Spoon into a greased muffin pan (muffin cups) filling each cup about 2/3 full. Bake in a preheated 400° oven for 25 minutes. Remove from pan and serve hot. Will make 6 large or 8 small muffins.

BROWN BREAD
(Boston style)

- 3/4 cup sifted flour
- 3/4 tsp. baking powder
- 3/4 cup white cornmeal
- 3/4 cup seedless raisins
- 1 tbsp. boiling water
- 2 1/4 cups buttermilk
- 3/4 tsp. salt
- 1 1/2 cup whole wheat flour
- 3/4 tsp. baking soda
- 2 eggs, slightly beaten
- 3/4 cup dark molasses

Grease two 1-pound coffee cans with unsalted shortening. In a medium-sized bowl, sift flour, baking powder, and salt together. Stir whole wheat flour, cornmeal, and raisins into dry ingredients. In a small dish, dissolve the soda in the boiling water. Mix buttermilk and molasses in a large bowl and stir in the baking soda mixture. Add the dry ingredients gradually, stirring till well mixed. Add eggs to batter and mix till thoroughly blended. Pour the batter into prepared cans, filling them only about two-thirds full. Cover cans with foil and tie foil securely with string. Place cans upright on a rack in a large, deep pot. Pour enough boiling water into pot to come to just about halfway up to the height of the cans. Place pot over moderate heat until water comes to a boil. Cover pot and reduce heat to moderately low. Steam for 3 hours. Add more boiling water to pot as is needed. Remove cans from water and cool for 15 minutes. Remove bread from cans. Cut into thin crosswise slices and serve with a breakfast spread, or even topped with cottage cheese, cream cheese, or sour cream.

SPOON-BREAD FLUFF

1 cup boiling water
1 cup white cornmeal
1/4 cup butter
1 tsp. salt
4 eggs, separated
1 cup milk
1 tbsp. sugar

Add cornmeal to boiling water. Stir till well mixed. Add butter; stir. Add milk; stir till smooth. Add beaten egg yolks, sugar, salt, and blend well. Beat egg whites till soft, fold into cornmeal mixture. Pour into well-greased casserole and bake in preheated 350° oven for 40 minutes. Serve at once.

CHEESE BREAD

1 cup scalded milk
2 1/3 cups sifted flour
4 tsp. baking powder
1 tsp. salt
1 cup shredded cheddar cheese
1 cup chopped dates
3/4 cup sugar
1/4 tsp. baking soda
1 egg, slightly beaten
1 tbsp. melted butter

Preheat oven to 325°. Grease a loaf-style pan. Pour the scalded milk over dates in a small bowl and let stand for 5 minutes. Meanwhile, sift flour, sugar, baking powder, baking soda, and salt together into a large mixing bowl. Fold cheese into dry ingredients. Make an inversion in the center. Add egg and butter to the date mixture and stir till well blended. Add date mixture to dry ingredients and stir until moistened. Pour mixture into the loaf pan and bake for 1 hour. Remove from oven when done and cool for 10 minutes. Wrap bread in foil and store in refrigerator. Keep there overnight. Makes one loaf.

MILK-AND-HONEY BREAD

1 cup sifted flour
3 tsp. baking powder
1/2 tsp. salt
1 cup graham flour
1/2 cup bran
1/2 cup chopped nuts
1 egg
1 cup milk
1/2 cup honey

Sift flour, baking powder, and salt together and mix with graham flour, bran, and nuts. Beat egg and add milk and honey. Add to dry ingredients and mix only a little. Pour into greased loaf pan and bake in 400° oven for 30 minutes. Will make 1 loaf.

BANANA-NUT BREAD

1/2 cup butter
2 cups sifted flour
2 tsp. baking powder
1/2 tsp. salt
1/2 cup chopped pecans
1 cup sugar
2 eggs
1/2 tsp. soda
1/4 tsp. nutmeg
1 cup mashed bananas

Cream the butter and sugar till smooth. Add eggs and mix thoroughly. Sift together flour, baking powder, salt, soda, and nutmeg. Add to creamed mixture with mashed bananas. Stir until dry ingredients are moistened. Then gently fold in pecans. Pour into a well-greased loaf pan. Bake at 350° for about 50 minutes. Makes one loaf.

MORNING MUFFINS

2 cups sifted flour
1 cup milk
3 tsp. baking powder
2 cups stale bread crumbs
1/2 tsp. salt
1 egg, slightly beaten
1/4 cup sugar
1/3 cup melted butter

Sift and measure flour. Add salt, baking powder, and sugar. Add 1 cup stale bread crumbs to flour mixture. Add the other cup to melted butter. Blend egg and milk. Add all at once to flour. Mix well. Fill greased muffin tin cups 2/3 full. Sprinkle any remaining crumbs over tops of muffins. Bake in preheated 400° oven for about 20 minutes. Serve while hot. Will make about 12 small muffins.

BLUEBERRY MUFFINS

2 cups sifted flour
1/3 cup sugar
1 egg, well beaten
1 cup frozen unsweetened blueberries
1 tbsp. sugar
3 tsp. baking powder
1 tsp. salt
1 cup milk
4 tbsp. melted butter
1 tsp. grated lemon rind

Sift flour, 1/3 cup sugar, baking powder, and salt into mixing bowl. Mix egg, milk, and butter in a small bowl. Stir lightly with fork until liquid is absorbed. Fold in blueberries. Spoon into greased muffin tins, filling to 2/3 full. Sprinkle with a mixture of the 1 tablespoon sugar and lemon rind. Bake in preheated 425° oven for about 20 minutes. Remove from oven and serve hot, with butter.

CRANBERRY BREAD

1/4 cup shortening
1/4 cup sugar
5 tsp. baking powder
1 tsp. salt
2 eggs, well beaten
2 cups sifted flour
2/3 cup milk
1 cup whole cranberry sauce

Cream together shortening and sugar. Fold in well-beaten eggs. Sift flour, baking powder, and salt together. Add sifted dry ingredients to shortening and sugar mixture with milk. Blend thoroughly. Add cranberry sauce. Grease a loaf pan and pour batter into it. Bake in preheated 400° oven for about 35-40 minutes. Makes 1 loaf.

COCONUT BREAD

3 cups flour
1 tsp. salt
1 cup grated coconut
1 1/2 cups milk
1 tbsp. grated orange rind
3 tsp. baking powder
1 cup sugar
1 egg, well beaten
1/2 cup chopped walnuts
1 tsp. vanilla

Stir flour, baking powder, salt, and sugar together in a large mixing bowl. Stir in coconut and orange rind. Combine egg with milk and mix with vanilla and walnuts. Stir milk mixture lightly but well into dry ingredients. Pour into a greased loaf pan. Bake for about 1 hour in a preheated 350° oven. Cool. Cut into thin slices and serve with plain yogurt.

HAWAIIAN BREAKFAST ROLLS

1/2 cup light brown sugar
3 tbsp. butter
1 medium can drained
crushed pineapple
2 tbsp. flour
1/2 cup pecan halves
8 brown-and-serve rolls

Blend together brown sugar and flour in a greased pie pan. Add butter, pineapple, and nuts. Heat mixture over low heat, till butter has melted. Place rolls upside down in mixture. Bake in preheated 400° oven for approximately 10 minutes. Remove and turn out on a serving plate. Brown rolls may be used also. These are especially good when topped with a little jam.

BABKA (a yeast bread)

4 cups flour
1 tsp. salt
1/2 tsp. cinnamon
1/2 cup butter
5 egg yolks, 1 kept separate
grated rind of 1 lemon
1 pkg. dry active yeast
1/2 cup sugar
1 1/4 cups milk
1 cup golden raisins
1/2 cup sliced almonds

Measure flour onto a piece of waxed paper. Combine 2 cups of flour and yeast, sugar, salt, cinnamon in a large mixing bowl. Stir well. Melt butter and add milk. Gradually add dry ingredients and use electric mixer to beat ingredients at low speed. After about 2 minutes of beating, add 4 egg yolks and 1 cup of flour. Beat at medium speed till yolks are well mixed into other ingredients. With a large spoon, gradually stir in the remaining flour to make a soft dough. Cover and let rise in a warm place, till doubled in size. Stir in raisins and lemon rind. Place in a well-greased tube-style pan; brush with egg yolk and 2 tablespoons of water. Sprinkle with almonds. Let stand to rise for about 1 hour. Bake in a preheated 350° oven for about 35 minutes. Turn out of pan; place right side up. Cool for about 1/2 hour before serving.

BREAKFAST CORN BREAD

1 1/2 cups scalded milk
1 1/2 cups white cornmeal
2 1/2 tsp. baking powder
1 egg, separated
1 tsp. salt
2 tsp. shortening

Mix milk with cornmeal and stir in salt and shortening. Cool, then add baking powder and egg yolk; mix well. Fold in stiffly beaten egg white. Pour into greased pan and bake in preheated 400° oven for 20 to 25 minutes. Will make 1 loaf.

FIG-OATMEAL MUFFINS

1 cup sifted flour
1/3 cup sugar
1 cup rolled oats
1/2 cup chopped dried figs
3 tbsp. cooking oil
3 tsp. baking powder
1/2 tsp. salt
1 egg, beaten
1 cup milk

Sift together flour, sugar, baking powder, and salt. Stir in oats and figs. Add eggs, milk, oil; stir. Fill greased tins 2/3 full. Bake in preheated 400° oven for about 15-17 minutes. Makes 12 muffins.

WHITE OVEN SCONES

- 2 cups flour
- 2 1/2 tsp. baking powder
- 1/2 tsp. salt
- 1 egg
- 2 tbsp. sugar
- 1/4 tsp. soda
- 1/4 cup butter
- 3/4 cup buttermilk

Mix flour, baking powder, soda, salt, and sugar together. Cut in butter; mix till crumbly. Beat eggs with a fork and combine with buttermilk. Mix quickly into dry ingredients with a fork. Turn dough out on a greased cookie sheet and pat into 2 circles about 1/2 inch thick. Cut each circle into 6 wedges with a knife dipped in flour. Prick with a fork. Bake in preheated 425° oven for about 12 minutes. Serve hot with butter and jam.

SUNRISE SCONES

- 2 cups flour
- 2 tbsp. sugar
- 1/4 cup sugar
- 1/3 cup shortening
- 1/2 cup milk
- ham and cherry filling
- 1 tbsp. baking powder
- 1 tsp. salt
- 1 egg
- 1 egg yolk
- 1 egg white

For ham and cherry filling

- 1 tbsp. butter
- 1 cup diced baked or broiled ham
- 1 can sweet pitted cherries
- 1/4 cup white sugar
- 1/4 tsp. allspice
- 1/2 cup water

Melt butter with sugar in skillet. Add water, ham, and cherries. Cook over low heat; cover and let steam for about 5 minutes. Add allspice. Let sit.

Directions for scones

Stir together flour, 1/4 cup sugar, baking powder, and salt. Cut in shortening until mixture is crumbly. Beat egg and yolk together. Blend in 1/4 cup milk. Add liquid all at once to flour mixture, stirring. Add more milk to make dough soft. Turn onto floured surface and knead for about 1 minute. Place on baking sheet; roll out to 1/2-inch-thick circle. Beat egg white till fluffy. Brush over top of dough. Sprinkle with 2 tablespoons sugar. Bake in preheated 425° oven for about 12 minutes. Split in half and fill with ham and cherry filling. Serve hot with cherry jelly.

LEMON HOT CROSS BUNS

3/4 cup hot lemon juice	**1/2 cup soft butter**
1/2 cup sugar	**1/2 tsp. cinnamon**
2 pkgs. active dry yeast	**1/2 tsp. salt**
1 cup light raisins	**3 eggs**
1/2 cup warm lemon juice	**4 cups unsifted flour**
1 tbsp. grated lemon rind	**glaze for buns**

Make glaze for buns by mixing together 1 cup confectioners' sugar and 1 tablespoon boiling water in a small mixing bowl; stir till smooth and creamy. Set aside. For buns, pour hot lemon juice over softened butter, sugar, cinnamon, and salt in a large bowl. Cool to lukewarm temperature. Dissolve yeast in the 1/2 cup of warm lemon juice. Add eggs to butter mixture. Mix thoroughly. Add enough flour to make dough soft. Place on a floured surface and knead till smooth adding raisins. Place in a large greased bowl. Cover and let rise until doubled in size; about two hours. Punch down and turn onto floured surface. Shape dough into 18 round balls. Place on greased baking sheets; cover and let rise till doubled in size; about 1 hour. With razor blade, cut a cross in top of each bun. Bake in a preheated 350° oven for about 20 minutes. Remove to room temperature and let cool. Drizzle glaze over each bun and serve.

PART VI

Toast

It's probably safe to say that most people like toast. Somehow, bread just tastes better when it is browned, hot, and spread with butter. But there are other ways to make toast a part of your morning meal.

One thing that seems to vary, even among toast lovers, is the consistency of the toast—or the surface hardness, if you please. Some people like soft, squishy toast. If you are one of them—then by all means, enjoy your toast. But don't assume that your guests will like it that way. Toast and fried eggs are two breakfast foods that should be personalized. And—don't forget the people who really do go for hard, dark toast, sparsely buttered. Many times, hard-toast lovers like to dunk their toast in coffee or hot milk, or whatever.

Then of course, there is french toast, long a breakfast favorite. French toast may also have many faces. Logically, just about any flavoring can be added to the egg mixture. So—try any favorites you may have—but please find the preferences of guests or family first. They'll appreciate it.

BRAN-ORANGE FRENCH TOAST

2 eggs
1/4 tsp. salt
1/2 cup confectioners' sugar
1 medium-sized can mandarin orange sections
1/4 cup orange juice
8 slices bran bread
1/4 cup shortening

Beat eggs with salt and orange juice. Dip bread slices into egg mixture. Brown on both sides in heated shortening. Sprinkle sugar over toast and garnish with drained mandarin orange slices (sections). Makes 4 servings.

BANANA FRENCH TOAST

2 beaten eggs
1 1/4 cups melted butter
8 slices white bread
1 tsp. nutmeg
2/3 cup milk
2 bananas, peeled

In a shallow bowl, combine 2 beaten eggs with 2/3 cup milk and 1 teaspoon nutmeg. Melt 1/4 cup butter in a skillet. Dip 8 slices of bread into egg mixture, turning to coat both sides. Brown bread on both sides. Keep warm in oven until all bread slices are browned. Place a layer of sliced bananas on 4 slices of french toast; cover with a second slice of toast. Melt remainder of 1 cup of butter, serve over toast. Makes 4 servings.

SURPRISE FRENCH TOAST

1 cup chopped cooked pitted prunes
2 tbsp. brown sugar
1 tbsp. frozen orange juice concentrate
1 egg
1/4 tsp. cinnamon
8 slices white bread
sour cream
2/3 cup milk

Preheat griddle. Blend 1 cup chopped pitted prunes, 2 tablespoons brown sugar, and 1 tablespoon of frozen concentrated orange juice (thawed). Spread between bread slices, making four sandwiches. Sauté in butter, turning to brown on both sides; next drizzle beaten egg onto each sandwich. Let sizzle for about 1 minute on each side. Serve immediately with sour cream. Makes 4 servings. Top with cinnamon.

FRENCH TOAST–MOLASSES STYLE

3 eggs, beaten
butter
8 slices white bread
2/3 cup milk
3 tbsp. molasses
1/6 tsp. nutmeg

In a mixing bowl, combine eggs, milk, molasses and nutmeg. Mix well, till all ingredients are well blended. In a frying pan, melt butter. Dip each slice of bread into egg mixture; fry. When toast is golden brown, remove from pan and serve. Butter may be applied as topping, or syrup. Serve warm. Will serve 8.

MAMUA FRENCH TOAST

1 can pineapple slices
butter
4 eggs, slightly beaten
1/2 tsp. salt
3/4 cup apricot jam
1 stick cinnamon
1 cup milk
8 slices white bread

Drain pineapple, reserving syrup for later use. In a saucepan, combine syrup, jam, 1/4 cup butter, and the cinnamon stick. Bring to a boil and simmer for 2 to 3 minutes. Meanwhile, sauté pineapple slices in butter and keep warm while preparing toast. Combine eggs, milk, and salt. Dip bread slices in egg mixture and sauté both sides in butter. Serve each slice of toast topped with a pineapple slice. Top with apricot or pineapple syrup. Will make 8 servings.

FRENCH TOASTED CHEESEWICH

3/4 cup applesauce
12 slices white bread
3 eggs, beaten
1/4 tsp. salt
1/2 tsp. cinnamon
butter
1/2 cup milk
12 slices cheddar cheese
2 tsp. sugar
syrup

Butter the bread well; spread with generous supply of applesauce. Place 2 cheese slices on each of 6 bread slices. Top with remaining bread. Blend the eggs, milk, sugar, salt, and cinnamon together. Dip sandwiches in egg mixture and grill in butter until golden brown in color. Then drizzle with desired amount of syrup. Will make 6 sandwiches.

STRAWBERRY FRENCH TOAST

2 cups cornflakes
1 box frozen strawberries, thawed
1/4 cup sugar
6 slices white bread cut crosswise into halves
3 eggs, slightly beaten
1/2 tsp. vanilla
1/3 cup half and half
dash of cinnamon
butter or margarine

Crush cornflakes into fine crumbs. Hull, wash, and crush strawberries, cover with sugar, and let stand for 30 minutes. Drain strawberries; reserve syrup. Combine eggs, half and half, vanilla, and 1/3 cup syrup; mix well. Place the bread in egg mixture; let stand till moistened well, turning once. Coat both sides of bread with cornflake crumbs. Brown bread slices in small amount of butter in frying pan. Add butter as needed to prevent sticking. Spread evenly with strawberries. Serve at once. Makes 6 servings.

BAKED FRENCH-STYLE TOAST

4 eggs, beaten
1 cup milk
6 slices dry bread
1/2 tsp. salt
1/2 cup butter, melted

Mix eggs, milk, and salt in a shallow dish. Dip bread into egg mixture and let liquid thoroughly saturate the bread. Place on a greased cookie sheet; drizzle the melted butter over the bread. Bake in a preheated 500° oven for about 7 minutes. Turn and bake for 3 additional minutes. Serve with hot butter. Makes 6 servings.

BRAN WAFFLE TOAST

1 egg, slightly beaten
3/4 cup milk
8 slices bran bread
soft butter
1/8 tsp. salt
maple syrup

Spread bread with butter. Combine egg, milk, and salt in mixing bowl. Dip each bread slice into mixture and then drain. Bake in a preheated 500° oven for 5 minutes. Serve drizzled with maple syrup. Serves 8.

CHEESE TOAST

2 eggs, beaten
3 tbsp. cream
2 cups grated American cheese
8 slices white bread
3 tbsp. flour
1/8 tsp. salt
1/8 tsp. pepper
cooking fat

Beat eggs, cream, salt, flour, cheese, and pepper together in mixing bowl. Spread onto slices of bread cut in 1-inch-thick strips. Fry in hot deep fat until bread is browned; placing cheese side down first, then turning over. Serves 8.

BUTTERSCOTCH NUT TOAST

1/4 cup butter, softened
1/2 cup brown sugar, packed firmly
8 slices bread, toasted
1/2 cup chopped pecans

Blend butter and sugar together in mixing bowl. Next, spread each slice of toast with 1 tablespoon butter mixture and sprinkle with pecans. Place toast spread side up on an ungreased cookie sheet. Toast under low broiler for about 5 minutes. Serve at once. Makes 4 servings. Note: other nuts may be substituted for the pecans.

SYRUP FOR FRENCH TOAST

1/2 cup white corn syrup
1/3 cup hot water
1/4 tsp. maple flavoring
1/4 cup brown sugar
1/8 tsp. salt

Mix all ingredients together in small saucepan. Heat over high heat for approximately 7 to 8 minutes; bring to a rapid boil. Remove from heat and let sit till cooled. Serve over any type of french toast Will make about 1 cup of syrup.

PART VII

Coffee Cakes

For those who like sweets, coffee cakes could prove to be the keynote of the breakfast menu. Here again, variations are easily made. However, those included here should certainly provide you with enough pleasing and compliment-baiting lovelies. Try them on guests, or on your family. You will be sure to please.

Coffee cakes should always be served, though not eaten, warm. That is to say most people know better than to bite right into a cake still moist and steaming from the oven. But don't let your guests eat cold coffee cake—that is unforgiveable! See to it that the coffee cake cools atop the oven (stove top) for about fifteen minutes (at least) before serving, so that it will still be warm when you serve it—but not hot.

If coffee cake is left over (from the morning meal) you might try wrapping it in foil or waxed paper and storing it in the freezer to use for snacks at a later date.

Check the beverage section of this book for tasty coffee, tea, or other hot and cold drinks to serve with your delightful morning coffee cakes.

CARAMEL BREAKFAST CAKE

2 tbsp. sugar
20 canned biscuits
1 cup caramel sauce
4 tbsp. chopped pecans
1/2 cup butter, melted

For caramel sauce

1/2 lb. bag caramels (28 pieces)
1/2 cup water

Place caramels and water in the top of a double boiler. Heat, stirring frequently until the caramels are melted and the sauce is smooth. Will make 1 cup of sauce.

Directions for Caramel Breakfast Cake

Sprinkle the sugar over bottom of a well-greased round cake pan. Cover with nuts, then pour on the caramel sauce. Separate the biscuits, and dip each in the melted butter. Place 15 of the biscuits, overlapping, around the outer edge of the pan. Use the remaining 5 biscuits to make an inner circle of overlapping biscuits. Bake in a hot (425°) oven for 15 minutes. Serve hot.

MAPLE-GLAZED CINNAMON LOAF

2 cans refrigerated Danish rolls with cinnamon and raisins
1/2 tsp. imitation maple flavoring
Maraschino cherries, drained
2 tbsp. chopped walnuts

Separate the 16 rolls. Stand one roll up, seam side down, against the end of an ungreased loaf pan. Stand two rolls side by side, seam sides down, against the first roll. And so continue placing rolls in pan in rows—singles, then pairs, till all the rolls are used. This should be baked in preheated 375° oven for 35 to 40 minutes or until center is done. Turn out onto plate, right side up, then frost while warm. To prepare frosting, thoroughly blend frosting from the biscuit rolls with maple flavoring. Spread on top of the loaf. Sprinkle with chopped nuts and garnish with maraschino cherries. Serve warm. Will make 1 loaf.

GINGER PEACHY ROLL

1 1/4 cups sugar
4 tbsp. butter
2 cups thinly sliced, peeled peaches
1 tbsp. ground ginger
1 tbsp. grated lemon peel
1 cup cold water
2 cups biscuit mix
1 tsp. nutmeg
1 tbsp. lemon juice
spiced sugar

For spiced sugar

1/8 tsp. nutmeg
1 tbsp. sugar
1/8 tsp. cinnamon
1/2 tsp. ground ginger

Mix all ingredients well, then set aside for later use for recipe.

Directions for Ginger Peachy Roll

Combine 1/2 cup sugar, 1/2 cup water, and 2 tablespoons butter in saucepan. Bring mixture to a bubbling boil, and stir until sugar is dissolved. Pour mixture (hot) into a large baking dish. Add remaining 1/2 cup water to biscuit mix and stir with a fork till mixed well. Round the dough into a ball, kneading several times. Sprinkle flour on counter top and roll biscuit ball into a long rectangle. Now, combine peaches with the nutmeg, the remaining 3/4 cup sugar, lemon juice, and peel. Distribute evenly over the dough. Dot with the remaining 2 tablespoons of butter, then sprinkle ginger over the surface. Roll the covered dough jellyroll fashion. Seal the edge by pressing firmly (the edge, not the ends). Use spatulas to lift the roll. Place seam side down in syrup in pan. Sprinkle the top with spiced sugar. Bake in preheated 400° oven for about 25 minutes. Top should be golden. Slice to serve after cooling. Spoon some of syrup from dish over roll.

YOGURT COFFEE CAKE

6 maple-frosted doughnuts
nutmeg
6 tbsp. lemon yogurt

Use a sharp knife to slit each end of doughnuts halfway through. Interlock the doughnuts, one to the other, in the fashion of a chain. Use a rolling pin to cause a dent or inversion in the center. Put doughnut chain into a long pan and place in 400° oven for only a few minutes. When removed from the oven, fill depression with spoonfuls of lemon yogurt. Top with nutmeg.

PEANUT BUTTER COFFEE CAKE

1/3 cup butter
1 egg
1 tsp. vanilla
1 cup sifted flour
1/2 tsp. soda
brown sugar topping
1/3 cup peanut butter
1/2 cup brown sugar, packed
1/2 cup dairy sour cream
1/2 tsp. baking powder
1/6 tsp. salt

For brown sugar topping

1/2 cup brown sugar, packed
1/4 tsp. cinnamon
1 tbsp. flour
3 tbsp. melted butter
1 tbsp. peanut butter

Blend sugar, flour, cinnamon, butter, and peanut butter till smooth and creamy. Use this mixture as topping for the cake.

For Peanut Butter Coffee Cake

Cream together butter, peanut butter, and sugar till smooth. Beat in egg and vanilla. Fold in the sour cream. Sift flour together with baking powder, soda, and salt. Stir gently into sour cream mixture. Turn into a greased square baking pan. Dot with the brown sugar topping and bake in a preheated 350° oven for approximately 30 minutes.

UPSIDE-DOWN COFFEE CAKE

1/3 cup butter
1/2 cup finely chopped pecans
1 tsp. cinnamon
1/2 tsp. baking powder
1/4 tsp. salt
2 eggs
1 tbsp. grated orange peel
1 1/2 cups brown sugar
1 tsp. nutmeg
1/2 tsp. soda
1 1/2 cups sifted flour
1/2 tsp. vanilla
1/4 cup butter
3/4 cup buttermilk

Melt 1/3 cup butter in square baking pan. Combine 1/2 cup sugar, pecans, cinnamon, and nutmeg. Sprinkle over butter. Sift together flour, baking powder, soda, and salt. Cream 1/4 cup butter in mixing bowl. Add remaining 1 cup brown sugar, mixing well. Beat in eggs, vanilla, and orange peel. Add sifted dry ingredients alternately with buttermilk. Spread batter carefully over topping in pan. Bake in preheated 350° oven for 45 to 50 minutes. Turn upside down on plate and serve warm.

ALOHA CHEESE RING

1 medium-sized can crushed pineapple
2 tbsp. sliced almonds
1 cup sugar
1 egg
1 tsp. salt
1 small pkg. cream cheese
2 tsp. vanilla
2 cups sifted flour
1 tsp. soda
1/2 cup dairy sour cream
pineapple drizzle

Directions for pineapple drizzle

1/2 cup drained crushed pineapple
1 cup sifted confectioners' sugar
1 tbsp. butter

Beat together pineapple, butter, and sugar. If a thicker glaze is desired, beat in an extra 1/2 cup of confectioners' sugar.

Directions for Aloha Cheese Ring

Drain pineapple, keeping the 1/2 cup syrup for the pineapple drizzle. Grease a tube-style pan, and then cover bottom with almonds. Beat cream cheese till soft. Mix in the sugar and vanilla. Blend egg in thoroughly. Sift the flour, soda, and salt together, and add alternately with the sour cream to the cheese mixture. Stir in the remaining pineapple, and then turn batter into pan. Bake in a preheated 350° oven for 45 minutes. Remove to wire rack and let stand for 10 minutes. Spread with pineapple drizzle.

CRISPY-TOPPED COFFEE CAKE

1 1/2 cups sifted flour
2 tbsp. instant coffee
1 tsp. baking powder
1/2 tsp. salt
3/4 cup buttermilk
1 egg, slightly beaten
3/4 cup sugar
1 tsp. cinnamon
1/2 tsp. soda
1/3 cup butter
1 tsp. vanilla

Sift together flour, sugar, coffee, cinnamon, baking powder, soda, and salt. Cut in butter. Reserve 1/3 cup of crumb mixture. Combine buttermilk, egg, and vanilla. Stir into remaining dry ingredients. Do not overbeat. Turn into a greased and floured square pan. Sprinkle batter with reserved crumbs. Bake in preheated 375° oven for 25 to 35 minutes. Serve warm. Will serve 9.

NUTTY PUFF CAKE

2 pkgs. biscuits
1/2 cup walnuts
2 tbsp. butter
1/2 cup honey

Arrange biscuits in a greased ringmold, overlapping the biscuits. Now spread the tops with softened butter. Then arrange walnuts on biscuits and top with honey. Bake in a preheated 350° oven for 15 to 20 minutes, or till done. Let stand about 5 minutes before removing from pan. Serves 8.

CITRUS COFFEE CAKE

1 pkg. coffee cake mix
1 tsp. grated lemon peel
1/2 cup confectioners' sugar
1 tsp. organge juice
1 egg
1 tsp. grated orange peel
1/2 cup milk

Add lemon and orange peels to coffee cake mix in a plastic bag; shake vigorously to mix. Put mixture into bowl and add liquid ingredients as directed. Pour into greased baking pan. Sprinkle topping included in the mix over batter (note: there is usually such a mix included; if not, mix dried bread crumbs and brown sugar together to use as a topping). Bake in preheated 375° oven for about 25 minutes. Meanwhile, beat together confectioners' sugar and orange juice till smooth. Drizzle over hot coffee cake. Cut into squares and serve when warm. Will provide 8 servings.

CARDAMOM-SESAME COFFEE CAKE

2 3/4 cups sifted flour
1 1/2 tsp. baking powder
1 tsp. crushed cardamom seed
1 tsp. sesame seed
1/4 cup finely chopped nuts
1/2 tsp. salt
1/2 cup butter
1/2 tsp. cinnamon
1 1/3 cups light cream
sugar

Mix together flour, baking powder, cardamom seed, sesame seed, and salt. Cut in butter until crumbly. Add cream and stir till well blended. Spread in greased square baking pan. Sprinkle with cinnamon mixed with sugar. Sprinkle with nuts and bake in 300° oven for 35 to 40 minutes. Serve when warm.

ORANGE BUTTER COFFEE CAKE SURPRISE

3 cups flour
1 tsp. salt
1/4 cup water
1 cup toasted flaked coconut
2 tbsp. grated orange peel
1 cup sugar
1 pkg. dry yeast
1/2 cup dairy sour cream
2 tbsp. melted butter
orange glaze

For orange glaze

6 tbsp. sugar
1 tbsp. orange juice
1/4 cup dairy sour cream
2 tbsp. butter

Combine sugar, sour cream, orange juice, and butter in a saucepan. Bring mixture to a boil. Let boil for 2 minutes, then remove from heat. Let cool. Mixture will become thick when cooled. Add to the top of coffee cake when it is done.

Directions for Orange Butter Coffee Cake Surprise

Combine 1 cup flour, 1/4 cup sugar, salt, and yeast (undissolved) in a large bowl and mix thoroughly. Next, combine water, sour cream, and butter in medium-sized saucepan. Heat over low heat till liquids are warm. Butter need not be melted. Add liquid to dry ingredients and beat 2 minutes at medium speed, if using electric beater. Add eggs and 1/2 cup flour or enough to make thick batter. Beat at high speed for 2 minutes.

Add additional flour to make a soft dough. Turn onto a lightly floured surface and knead until smooth and firm, about 10 minutes. Place dough in a greased bowl, turning to grease top. Cover and let rise until doubled in bulk; about 1 hour should be sufficient. Punch dough down, and turn onto a floured surface. Roll into a long rectangle. Brush dough with melted butter.

Mix the remaining 3/4 cup sugar, 3/4 cup coconut, and orange peel. Spread filling over the dough. Roll dough in jellyroll fashion from the side and seal seams tightly. Place seam side down in a greased pan (tube-style). Cover and let rise in a warm place till doubled in bulk; about 1 hour. Bake in preheated 350° oven for 30 minutes or till cake feels firm to touch. Remove from oven and pour orange glaze over coffee cake. Sprinkle with the remaining coconut. Serve warm. Should provide about 12 slices.

PEAR CRUNCHY COFFEE CAKE

1 large can pear halves
1/3 cup orange marmalade
2 1/2 cups biscuit mix
1/2 tsp. cinnamon
1 cup whole bran cereal
twists of orange peel and pecans
2 tbsp. butter
1/4 cup shortening
1/4 cup sugar
1/4 tsp. nutmeg
2 eggs

Drain pears, reserving syrup. Melt the butter in a square cake pan. Stir in marmalade and spread evenly over the bottom of the pan. Arrange pear halves, cut sides down, over marmalade. Cut the shortening into the biscuit mix. Stir in sugar, spices, and bran cereal. Beat eggs with 1 cup reserved pear syrup. Pour into biscuit mix and stir until blended. Pour carefully over the pears. Bake in a preheated 400° oven for 20 to 25 minutes. Let the cake stand for 5 or 10 minutes before turning out onto a platter. Serve warm with garnish of orange twists and pecans. Makes 8 to 10 servings.

COFFEE CAKE LE CREME

1 cup dairy sour cream
1 tsp. salt
2 tbsp. butter
1 pkg. cake yeast
4 1/2 cups sifted flour
1/3 cup brown sugar, firmly packed
1/3 cup chopped nuts
3 tbsp. sugar
1/8 tsp. soda
1/3 cup warm water
1 egg
1/3 cup butter
1 tsp. cinnamon
1/4 tsp. nutmeg

Scald sour cream. Stir in 3 tablespoons sugar, salt, soda, and the 2 tablespoons butter. Cool to lukewarm. Measure warm water into large bowl, sprinkle or crumble in yeast, and stir till dissolved. Add lukewarm cream mixture, egg, and 1 3/4 cups flour. Beat for 2 minutes at medium speed on mixer. Add 1 3/4 cups flour to make soft dough. Turn onto floured surface and knead until smooth and firm.

Put dough into greased pan. Cream 1/3 cup butter. Blend sugar into mixture. Add remaining 1 cup flour, cinnamon, nuts, and nutmeg. Stir till well mixed. Sprinkle over dough. Let rise in a warm place till doubled in bulk. Bake in preheated 375° oven for about 30 minutes, or till done. Cool slightly in pan and drizzle with confectioners' sugar, if desired.

CANDY PEANUT RING

3 tbsp. butter
2/3 cup crushed peanut brittle
1/3 cup flaked coconut
2 tbsp. grated orange rind
20 canned biscuits

Measure butter into tube-style mold. Place in preheated oven for a few minutes until butter is melted. Remove pan from oven and tip mold to coat the bottom of the pan with butter. Sprinkle coconut evenly around the mold and press it against the bottom of the pan. Blend peanut brittle and orange rind; spoon over coconut in mold. Separate biscuits and stand upright in single row around the prepared mold. Bake in a 400° oven for 10 to 12 minutes or till top is browned. Turn out immediately onto a serving plate. To serve, pull biscuits apart with two forks. Serve hot.

GRECIAN COFFEE CAKE

1 pkg. apricot nut bread mix
1 tsp. cornstarch
1 tbsp. apricot brandy
1 cup golden raisins
1/2 cup apricot nectar

Prepare mix as box directs, adding raisins. Turn into tube-style mold, greased and floured. Bake at 350° for approximately 1 hour. Cool for 10 minutes before turning onto plate.

Meanwhile, combine cornstarch, apricot nectar, and the brandy in a saucepan. Heat, stirring constantly. Mixture will be thick. Prick surface of the coffee cake with a toothpick in many places. Then spoon the hot sauce over the cake, allowing mixture to soak in. The coffee cake is best when served warm.

PEACH COFFEE CAKE SWIRL

1/4 cup sugar
2 tsp. cinnamon
1 pkg. yellow cake mix
1 2/3 cups peaches, sliced
3 eggs

Blend sugar and cinnamon. Grease a tube-style pan and dust with about 1 tablespoon sugar-cinnamon. Save remainder for the coffee cake. Blend cake mix, peaches, and eggs until moistened. Beat as directed on the package. Reserve 1 1/2 cups batter. Pour remaining batter into the pan. Sprinkle with remaining sugar-cinnamon mixture, then top with the rest of the batter. Bake in preheated 350° oven for 35 to 45 minutes, or until done. Cool cake in pan, top side up, for 15 to 20 minutes. Turn out on a serving plate. Serve warm.

DAISY CAKES
(yeast bread)

5 1/2 cups unsifted flour
1 tbsp. grated lemon peel
1 tsp. salt
2 pkgs. active try yeast
confectioners' sugar
lemon filling
3/4 cup sugar
1/2 cup milk
1/2 cup butter
3 eggs
1/2 cup water

Directions for lemon filling

2 pkgs. cream cheese
2 tbsp. sugar
yellow food coloring
1 egg yolk
1 tsp. grated lemon
lemon juice

Blend together cream cheese and egg yolk. Add sugar, lemon and a few drops of food coloring. Stir in lemon juice. Set aside.

Directions for Daisy Cakes

Mix 1 1/2 cups flour with sugar, salt, lemon peel, and undissolved active dry yeast together in a large mixing bowl. In a saucepan, combine milk, water, and butter. Heat over low heat till liquids are warm. Add to dry ingredients and beat for 2 minutes at medium speed with electric beater. Stir in additional flour (enough to make a soft dough). Turn out onto floured surface. Knead till smooth; about 10 minutes. Cover and let rise in a warm place till dough has doubled in bulk; 1 1/2 hours or so.

Punch dough down. Turn out onto lightly floured surface. Divide dough in half. Roll one half into a rectangle. Cut into 14 strips about 1 inch wide. Twist two strips together; hold one end of twist firmly and wind dough to form a coil; tuck end underneath. Repeat till all strips are used. Place one coil in center of greased cookie sheet. Place remaining coils around the center one, so that all coils are touching. Repeat with remaining dough. Cover; let rise in a warm place (free from draft) till doubled in bulk; about 1 hour.

Press a deep indention into the center of each coil (roll) making an indention of about an inch. Spoon the prepared lemon filling mixture into each impression.

Bake in preheated 375° oven for 25 to 30 minutes, or until done. Remove from oven and cool. Frost with confectioners' sugar mixed with a little water. Will make 2 coffee cakes.

APRICOT COFFEE CAKE

- 1/2 cup butter
- 3/4 cup apricot preserves
- 1 cup brown sugar, firmly packed
- 1 tbsp. grated orange peel
- 1 1/2 cups sifted flour
- 1/2 tsp. baking powder
- 2 eggs
- 1 tsp. lemon juice
- 1/2 tsp. soda
- 1/2 tsp. vanilla
- 1/4 tsp. salt
- 3/4 cup buttermilk

Preheat oven to 350°. Place 1/4 cup butter in square pan and place in oven. Spoon preserves into the hot melted butter and then spread in pan with the back of a spoon. Sprinkle with lemon juice.

Cream remaining 1/4 cup butter, gradually adding the brown sugar and beat till fluffy. Beat in eggs one at a time. Blend in orange peel and vanilla. Sift flour together with baking powder, soda, and salt. Add to creamed mixture alternately with buttermilk, beginning and ending with the dry ingredients. Spread batter carefully over topping in pan. Bake at 350° for 45 to 50 minutes. Let stand in pan for 10 minutes before turning out onto serving plate. Will serve 8.

PEANUT-APPLE COFFEE CAKE

- 1 1/2 cups sifted flour
- 1/6 tsp. salt
- 1 egg, beaten
- 1/2 cup chopped salted peanuts
- 1/2 cup sugar
- 2 tsp. baking powder
- 1/2 cup milk
- 3 tbsp. peanut oil
- coffee cake topping

For coffee cake topping

- 1/4 cup flour
- 1 tsp. cinnamon
- 2 apples
- 1/4 cup sugar
- 1/4 cup butter

For topping, mix together flour, sugar, and cinnamon. Cut or rub butter into mixture until crumbly. Peel and core apples; slice thin.

Directions for Peanut-Apple Coffee Cake

Blend oil, eggs, sugar, salt, and milk together in a large mixing bowl. In another bowl, sift together flour, baking powder. Add to other mixture. Blend in peanuts. Knead dough briefly. Place in loaf pan. Spread thinly sliced apples over dough. Add topping to the surface. Bake in preheated 350° oven for 30 to 35 minutes, or till done. Cool before serving.

COFFEE CAKE LE RAISIN

1/3 cup butter
1 tsp. cinnamon
1/2 cup finely chopped pecans
1 1/2 cups sifted flour
1/2 tsp. baking powder
1/4 tsp. vanilla
1 tsp. grated orange peel
1 1/2 cups raisins (dark)
2 eggs
1 1/2 cups brown sugar
1 tsp. nutmeg
1/2 tsp. soda
3/4 cup buttermilk
1 cup half and half
1 tsp. milk
1/2 cup raisins (golden)
1/4 cup chopped apples

Cream eggs into 1/3 cup butter. Add vanilla, milk, buttermilk, cinnamon, nutmeg, and sugar. Into another bowl, put sifted flour, baking powder, salt, and soda. Combine mixtures. Add half and half. Knead dough. Grease a large cake pan and flatten out dough in it. Cover surface with raisins, pecans, apples, and orange peel. Then dot with remaining 1/4 cup butter. Garnish with a little extra cinnamon and nutmeg. Bake in preheated 305° oven for approximately 1 hour. Cool slightly in the pan before cutting. Cut with a very sharp knife; the top section may be extremely sticky, making cutting a bit difficult. Serve warm; plain, or with a dab of yogurt.

PART VIII

Jellies, Jams, and Preserves

Take my word for it, there is really no better way for a hostess (or wife and mother) to show her creativity, ingenuity, and a touch of the old-fashioned virtues, than by making jellies, jams, and preserves. This is a highly personal way to show hospitality to guests and family. And the choice is endless.

For example: try experimenting with combinations; any kind you happen to like. But remember, this is one avenue of breakfast cookery that needs special types of equipment. You will need jelly jars, paraffin for the sealing, and a few large pots and pans if you want to make jelly, rather than some of the easier-to-make spreads. Please keep in mind here that this author does not claim to present the key to jelly-making; if you are a novice, if you are at all insecure in the process of making jellies, then by all means seek help from other texts or from friends or family and use this section as a recipe base rather than a "how-to."

At any rate, even those who have the know-how can experience a memory gap, so please keep this in mind: some fruits have more natural pectin than others; pectin that makes for proper jelling. Here are those fruits that do not have the necessary pectin and will need an added commerical substitute: cherries, peaches, pineapple, rhubarb, strawberries.

These are the fruits that have the necessary pectin for jelling and do not need a substitute: currants, gooseberries, tart apples, crab apples, blackberries, grapes, loganberries, plums, quinces, and raspberries.

When making jelly, be sure to mind the sugar factor. Many times, jelly-making is a failure because too much sugar is added. Therefore, do not add any more sugar to the recipe than is called for. If anything, add a little less.

You will notice that jams take less sugar than jellies or the preserves do. They are also easier to make, if care is taken that the mixture is not burned on the bottom of the pan while cooking. Therefore, be sure to watch the heat carefully. In making preserves, be sure that all hard fruit is sufficiently boiled in heavy syrup.

As far as preparation for "canning" is concerned, there are really only a few basic rules that must be followed, but followed closely. First of all, make sure that all fruit mixtures have been cooked with enough heat to destroy any germs or organisms. Then see to it that the jars are sealed well so that no spoiling will take place. The old-fashioned (and fondly remembered) fruit cellar is well in our past, but it is still wise to keep jars in a cool, damp place for storage until used.

Make sure that all jars are sterilized before use! Do this by filling a pressure cooker with boiling water to the bottom of the rack. Then put the jars in and heat for seven minutes. When enough steam has been released from the cooker, open the pan, and remove jars with a pot-holder. Place the jars upside down on the sink counter or other available space. Let them cool and they will be ready for use. Tops for jars may be sterilized in the same manner.

DIETER'S GRAPE JAM

2 tsp. unflavored gelatin
3 lbs. concord grapes
2 tbsp. liquid artificial sweetener
1 tbsp. cold water
1/3 cup water

Soften gelatin in cold water. Wash grapes and place in kettle with water. Cook over medium heat, being sure to stir frequently, till grapes are soft. Remove from heat; force grapes through food mill to remove seeds and skins. Measure, add water, if necessary, to make 4 cups of pulp. Add sweetener and softened gelatin. Return to heat and continue to cook for 1 minute. Remove from heat; ladle into half-pint jars, cover, and store. Makes 4 half pints, each tablespoon measuring 9 calories, 2.0 grams carbohydrate. With sugar, the same recipe would measure 37 calories per tablespoon.

LOW-CALORIE PLUM JAM

2 tsp. unflavored gelatin
2 1/2 lbs. plums
4 tbsp. liquid artificial sweetener
1 tbsp. cold water
1/2 cup water

Soften gelatin in cold water. Wash fruit, remove stems, halve the plums, and pit them. Place in a kettle with water. Cook over medium heat, stirring occasionally until plums are soft. Crush lightly. Measure fruit, add water, if necessary, to make 4 cups of pulp. Add sweetener and softened gelatin. Return to heat and continue to cook for 1 minute. Remove from heat; ladle into half-pint jars, cover and store. Makes 4 half pints, each tablespoon measuring 9 calories, 2.0 grams carbohydrate. With sugar the same recipe would measure 37 calories per tablespoon.

GOOSEBERRY PRESERVES

1 lb. green gooseberries
1 1/4 lbs. sugar

Stem berries, remove blossom ends, and wash fruit in cold water. Half cover the gooseberries with water and scald fruit till skins are soft. Add sugar to hot mixture. Bring quickly to boiling point and cook till clear. Pour into jars; cover and store. Will make 1 pint.

CRANBERRY-LEMON PRESERVES

2 cups sugar
1 pkg. frozen unsweetened cranberries
1 cup orange juice
2 lemons

In a medium-sized saucepan, mix the sugar and orange juice and bring to a boil. Cut lemons into thin slices, remove seeds, and simmer for 5 minutes, or until peels are wilted. Now add the cranberries and simmer the mixture for 5 minutes, or until the cranberries are tender, yet firm. Let the cranberries cool in the syrup; then spoon into jars. Seal jars and store in refrigerator until ready to serve. Makes approximately 3 pints.

DONNA-ROSE JAM

2 cups rhubarb, diced
2 cups ripe strawberries
4 cups sugar
2 cups rose petals

Wash petals well. Halve berries. Pour hot water over rhubarb to scald. Drain rhubarb promptly. Cover it, berries, and petals with sugar and let stand for approximately 24 hours. Cook until the syrup drops from the spoon in a sheet, rather than in drops. Stir frequently to prevent floating fruit. Pour into sterilized jars and seal. Will make 4 to 6 glasses of jam.

THE SPREAD WITH SOMETHING EXTRA

(Author's note: This is quite a "sophisticated" spread for the breakfast table, but an exciting change from the more ordinary spread.)

1 envelope unflavored gelatin
3 tbsp. sugar
4 tbsp. instant coffee
1/4 cup domestic white creme de cacao
1/4 cup cold water
1 1/2 cups boiling water
dash of nutmeg

In a one-quart bowl, sprinkle gelatin over cold water and allow to soften for about five minutes. Add sugar, dash of nutmeg, coffee, and boiling water; stir to dissolve. Stir in creme de cacao. Put mixture into deep bowl and store in refrigerator. Cool before serving. If desired, fold in a little whipped cream before serving. Use as a topping for pancakes, toast, or as a scoop serving in hot coffee or cocoa on a winter morning.

APRICOT-PINEAPPLE JAM

7 cups fresh apricots
3 cups crushed pineapple
5 cups sugar

Wash and slice apricots. Mix pineapple (and juice) with sugar. Cook in large saucepan until thick and well jelled. This time period should be about 25 minutes, but no longer. Pour into hot, sterilized jars, and seal. Will make approximately 5 pints.

FIG-STRAWBERRY PRESERVES

3 cups mashed figs
2 pkgs. strawberry gelatin
3 cups sugar

Thoroughly mix figs, gelatin, and sugar in a large saucepan. Bring to boil over medium heat, and then boil for 3 minutes, stirring only occasionally. When the mixture has thickened, pour quickly into glasses. Makes about 6 medium-sized glasses of preserves.

TANGERINE RELISH

3 tangerines
1/3 cup seedless dark raisins
2 whole cloves
1 tbsp. water
1/2 cup diced celery
1/3 cup chopped walnuts
1/2 cup brown sugar
1 stick cinnamon
1 1/2 cups water
1 tbsp. cornstarch
1 large apple, diced

Grate peel from tangerines to yield 2 teaspoons. Remove peel and separate tangerines into segments, removing any seeds. Combine raisins, brown sugar, cinnamon stick, cloves, grated tangerine peel, and 1 1/2 cups water in a large saucepan. In small saucepan, dissolve cornstarch with 1 tablespoon water. Add to other mixture, and bring to boil. Cook for 10 minutes over medium heat, stirring frequently. Add tangerine segments, nuts, and celery.

Simmer about 1 1/2 minutes until heated through. This mixture may be put into jars, sealed, and stored—or served when cooled. This relish is particularly tasty with breakfast salads, or even as a topping for cereals, rather than using sugar or syrup.

PLUM-WINE JELLY

2 cups sliced purple plums
1 cup honeydew melon balls
1 stick cinnamon, broken
1 pkg. strawberry gelatin
3/4 cup tokay wine
2 cups water
5 whole cloves
1/2 lemon, sliced
2 tsp. lemon juice

Combine sliced plums and melon balls in a shallow dessert bowl. Combine 1 cup water, cloves, cinnamon, and lemon. Bring to a boil. Strain and pour over gelatin. Stir till dissolved. Add the remaining 1 cup water, the lemon juice, and wine. Pour over fruit in bowl. Chill until set. Jelly will be soft, not firm. Spoon into jars and cover; seal. Will make approximately 3 to 4 jars.

BANANA JAM SPREAD

6 medium-ripe bananas
1 jar maraschino cherries
1 medium can crushed pineapple
5 cups sugar
1 bottle pectin

Crush bananas in a saucepan with fork. Add drained and chopped cherries, pineapple (with syrup), sugar; mix well. Bring to a boil over medium heat. Boil for 1 minute. Remove from the heat, stir in pectin. Let stand for 3 to 5 minutes. Ladle into jelly glasses. Makes approximately 10 glasses.

LIME AND NECTARINE JAM

2 1/4 lbs. nectarines
6 1/2 cups sugar
1 two-inch cinnamon stick
4 medium-sized limes
1/4 tsp. salt
1/2 bottle pectin

Chop the nectarines to measure 4 cups. Coarsely grate the peel from 1 lime, then squeeze 2 tablespoons juice. The remaining three limes should be peeled and the pulp grated and chopped. Combine nectarines, grated peel, lime juice, lime pulp, sugar, salt, and cinnamon in large saucepan. Bring to a full, rolling boil and have the mixture boil hard for 1 minute, stirring constantly. Remove from heat and immediately stir in pectin. Skim off foam with metal spoon. Stir and skim 5 minutes, to prevent fruit from floating. Ladle into jars, and cover. Makes 10 medium-sized glasses.

CRANBERRY-APPLE BUTTER

3 lbs. apples (about 12)
3 cups sugar
1/2 tsp. ground cloves
1 lb. fresh cranberries
1 tsp. ground cinnamon
1/2 tsp. nutmeg

Cut the apples into quarters; pare and core. Combine all the ingredients in a large kettle and boil, stirring often, till apples soften into pulp and the mixture becomes thick (about 20 or 25 minutes). Spoon while hot into glasses. Cover with paraffin. Serve (when cooled) on bread, or use as a topping for pancakes, waffles, oatmeal, or other hot cereals, such as cream of wheat, cream of rice, etc.

STRAWBERRY BUTTER

2 cups crushed strawberries (unsweetened)
syrup drained from fruit
1 cup softened butter
4 tbsp. confectioners' sugar

Whip butter till light and frothy. Add sugar gradually, beating thoroughly. Add strawberries and syrup slowly, beating constantly. Chill in refrigerator. Makes approximately 2 to 3 cups.

STRAWBERRY-MINT JAM

1 qt. ripe strawberries
2 tbsp. chopped mint
1/2 bottle pectin
4 cups sugar
juice from 1 lemon

First, strawberries should be washed and stems removed. Crush berries (only a few at a time). When that is finished, measure 1 3/4 cups into a large bowl and add the chopped mint. Now prepare the jam. Thoroughly mix sugar into the fruit; let stand for approximately 10 minutes. Then squeeze the juice from 1 lemon; measure 2 tablespoons and add to fruit pectin in a small bowl. Stir into fruit. Continue stirring the mixture for about 3 minutes. A few sugar crystals will remain. Ladle into jars and cover; store, or place in small separate bowls and store in refrigerator, if canning is not desired. Canned, the mixture will yield approximately 3 glasses.

WINE JELLY

1 envelope unflavored gelatin
3 tbsp. sugar
juice of 1/2 lemon
1 cup water
1 cup dry white wine

Soften gelatin in 2 tablespoons cold water. Bring remainder of water to a boil and stir in gelatin and sugar till dissolved. Cool gelatin slightly, then stir in wine and lemon juice. Turn into a mold, and cool in the refrigerator. If desired, mixture may be put into glass jars and stored for later use. Serve as a spread on toast, or as a "floating spoonful" in coffee.

PEACH CONSERVE

4 cups chopped cantaloupe
6 cups sugar
1/4 cup lemon juice
1/2 tsp. cloves
4 cups chopped peaches
1/4 tsp. salt
1/2 tsp. nutmeg
3/4 cup chopped walnuts

Combine cantaloupe and peaches. Let them simmer in a deep saucepan for about 20 minutes, stirring occasionally to prevent sticking. Add sugar, salt, and lemon juice and boil till thick. Stir the mixture every so often. Add nutmeg, cloves, and walnuts and boil for 3 minutes longer. Ladle the mixture into jars; cover and store in a cool place. Makes approximately 4 to 5 pints.

GRAPEFRUIT MARMALADE

2/3 cup thinly sliced grapefruit peel
1 1/3 cups chopped grapefruit pulp (about 1 fruit)
4 cups sugar
4 cups water

Cover peel with water; bring to a boil and keep boiling for about 10 minutes. Drain. Repeat this method a few times—two or three. Add the chopped pulp and 4 cups of water to drained peel, cover and let stand for approximately 12 to 18 hours in a cool place.

Cook rapidly until peel is tender, about 40 minutes. Measure fruit and liquid. Add 1 cup of sugar for each cup of fruit mixture. Bring slowly to a boiling point, stirring until sugar dissolves. Cook rapidly almost to jelling point, about 30 to 35 minutes. Stir occasionally to prevent sticking. Pour (boiling hot) into jars; cover and store. Makes about 1 1/2 pints.

LIME MARMALADE

1 1/2 cups cut-up lime
1/3 cup light corn syrup
2/3 cup water
2/3 cup sugar

To prepare fruit, wash and dry. Peel half the fruit. Slice peeled and unpeeled fruit and cut into quarters. Then measure. Bring water, sugar, and corn syrup to a boil. Add fruit and boil until mixture begins to jell Ladle mixture into jars, cover, and store. Will make approximately 1 1/2 pints

PEAR-RAISIN SPREAD

4 cups chopped pear slices
4 cups cooked raisins
2 cups chopped, unpeeled oranges
2 lemons, thinly sliced
2/3 cup sugar
1 qt. water

Combine lemon, orange, and raisin combinations in saucepan with water. Cook at low-to-medium heat until peel is tender and raisins are very soft (time should be about 20 minutes). Cool mixture. Add pears and sugar Bring to a boil slowly, stirring until sugar dissolves. Cook rapidly to jelling point, about 20 minutes, stirring frequently. Let stand at room temperature to cool. Ladle into jars; cover and store. Will make approximately 4 jars. This spread is a good topping for cooked cereal or toast

SUN-COOKED PRESERVES

1 1/2 lbs. strawberries
6 cups sugar
1 1/2 cups raspberries
3 cups water

Wash berries, removing green tops. Weigh them. Combine sugar and water and cook until mixture begins to thicken. Remove from heat Add berries and let stand overnight. Then skim berries from syrup and place in deep platters in a single layer. Cook syrup again and pour over the berries. Cover with a piece of cheesecloth and let stand in direct sunlight for 3 to 4 days. When syrup has become thickened, pour into jars, and cover. Since any dampness may cause some mold to form quickly on this type of preserves, they must be brought indoors each night. If the sun does not shine, cooking must be finished indoors. Makes 4 pints.

THYME AND GRAPE JELLY

1/2 cup boiling water
1 tbsp. dried thyme
1/2 cup liquid pectin
1 1/2 cups grape juice
3 cups sugar

Pour boiling water over thyme, cover, and then let stand for about 5 minutes. Strain through a fine cheesecloth. Add enough water to make 1/2 cup. Add grape juice and sugar and heat to a boiling point. Add pectin, stirring constantly. Boil hard for 1/2 minute. Remove from heat, skim, and pour into glasses. Seal, then store. This spread is delicious with english muffins.

ROSELLE JELLY

2 cups roselle juice
1 1/2 cups sugar
1 cup roselles
2 tsp. lemon juice
1/2 bottle liquid pectin

Wash roselles, cover with water, and cook till tender. Strain through jelly bag. Measure juice and boil for about 5 minutes. Add lemon juice, pectin, and sugar and cook until it sheets from the spoon. Skim, then pour into jelly glasses. Will make 2 glasses of jelly.

GRAPE BUTTER

4 lbs. ripe purple grapes
2 cups sugar
1 cup water

Wash and stem grapes. Add water and cook till tender. Rub grapes through a sieve, then measure the pulp and add 1/2 the volume of sugar. Cook till thick and clear. Pour into pint jars (or into bowl) and let set in refrigerator. Makes 3 jars.

PEACH BUTTER

4 lbs. peaches
2 cups sugar
2 cups water

Peel and slice peaches, discarding stones. Cook fruit in water till tender. Rub through sieve, measure pulp and add 1/2 volume of sugar. Cook till mixture is very thick and clear. Let set for a few minutes at room temperature before pouring into jars. Will make 3 pints.

ARIZONA DESERT PRESERVES
(cactus)

Prickly pears, the basis of this type of preserves, may not be had in all parts of the country. However, Mexican markets have them; also markets in California or the Southwest. If the fruit is scarce, it may be eaten in the following manner: sliced lengthwise, topped off with lemon juice and sugar. However, if many are available, the following recipe may be used:

3 cups unpeeled chopped oranges
1 qt. chopped, seeded prickly pears (about 9)
2 lemons, thinly sliced
1 qt. water
6 cups sugar

Combine lemon, orange, and water in saucepan. Cover and let stand for 12 to 18 hours in a cool place. Cook rapidly until the peel is tender, about 30 minutes. Cool. Add pears and sugar. Bring to a boil slowly, stirring till sugar dissolves. Cook rapidly to jelling point, about 20 minutes, stirring often. Pour boiling hot into jars and seal. Will make approximately 3 pints.

PEAR BUTTER

8 cups pears, peeled, cored, coarsely chopped
whole peel from 1/2 lemon
1/6 tsp. salt
3 tbsp. lemon juice
4 1/2 cups sugar
1/2 tsp. ground ginger

To retard darkening, drop each pear as it is peeled and cored, into an ascorbic acid mixture solution (two or three teaspoons of mixture to one quart cold water) or use a weak brine (one tablespoon salt to one quart water). Now, thoroughly drain pears. Do not chop lemon peel. Mix all ingredients and boil rapidly. Stir often till mixture is thick, then stir almost constantly till there is very little liquid left. Discard lemon peel. Pour hot mixture into jars. Makes approximately 3 pints.

CHERRY-NUT PRESERVES

2 lbs. pitted tart cherries
3 cups sugar
1/2 cup chopped walnuts

Add sugar to cherries and heat quickly to boiling point. Cook rapidly till fruit is clear and skimming is necessary. Let cool. Fold in nuts. Pour into jars, cover, and store. Makes 2 pints.

APPLE AND PLUM BUTTER

3 lbs. apples
1 lb. plums
1 cup water
2 cups sugar

Wash fruit well. Quarter and core apples and cut the plums into halves. Combine fruit and water and cook till the mixture is tender. Rub through a sieve. Now measure pulp and add 1/3 of the sugar. Cook till mixture begins to thicken; add remainder of sugar. Stir constantly, to keep mixture from sticking to bottom of the pan. Let mixture set, then pour into jars. Cover and put into refrigerator to store. Makes approximately 3 pints.

PRESERVED GINGER

1 lb. fresh ginger roots
1 lb. sugar
1 1/2 cups water

Scrub roots of fresh green ginger thoroughly, using a brush. Pare with a very sharp knife, and place the roots at once in cold water. Rinse well and place in fresh cold water. Let stand overnight. Drain and weigh ginger, place it in a preserving kettle, and cover it with cold water. When the water is boiling, skim out the ginger and place it again in cold water. When quite cool, return to the kettle, add more cold water, and when water is boiling, skim the ginger out and lay it in cold water, as done before. Do this three times, or until ginger is tender.

Boil sugar and water together for ten minutes. Drain ginger and add it to the syrup. Then bring it quickly to boiling point; remove from heat and let it stand overnight. Drain off syrup, let it come to a boil, and repeat the first process.

Drain off syrup again, heat to boiling point. Add ginger and simmer until clear. Pour into jars, cover, and store. Ginger will be ready for use in two weeks.

KUMQUAT PRESERVES

3 lbs. kumquats
3 1/2 cups water
6 cups sugar

Make a deep slit in one end of each of the kumquats and cover with cold water, allowing to stand thusly for 24 hours, or at least overnight. To prepare, heat to boiling and cook till tender. Add the sugar and cool until mixture is thick. Pour into jars, cover, and store. Will make 4 pints.

LOQUAT JELLY

5 lbs. ripe loquats
1 cup water
5 1/2 cups sugar
1 pkg. pectin
1/2 cup lemon juice

Wash and stem loquats and remove seeds. Combine fruit and water in a saucepan; cover and simmer for about 15 minutes. Strain juice through a jelly bag. Measure 3 1/2 cups of juice into a large kettle. If the loquat juice does not measure 3 1/2 cups, fill the last cup or fraction with water. Add lemon juice. Add pectin and stir well. Place over high heat and bring to a boil, stirring constantly. Stir in sugar and continue to stir while bringing mixture to a full and rolling boil; boil for 2 minutes. Remove from heat; let boiling subside. Skim carefully. Pour into jelly glasses. Cover and seal. Makes approximately 4 pints.

FIG-ORANGE JAM

1 qt. sliced peeled figs
1 orange
lemon juice
chopped preserved ginger
3 cups sugar

Place figs in large saucepan. Squeeze orange, and add juice to figs. Grind or chop orange peel very fine, and add to figs. Bring to a boil slowly, then boil rapidly until peel is tender, stirring occasionally. Add sugar, lemon juice, and ginger (to taste). Cook, stirring frequently, until a few drops on a cold plate congeal quickly. Ladle into jelly glasses and seal. Makes about 4 pints.

PICKLED FIGS

6 qts. figs
8 cups brown sugar, firmly packed
2 tsp. whole cloves
1 qt. vinegar
1 3-inch cinnamon stick
salt

Wash figs. Boil for 15 minutes in salted water (about 1 tablespoon salt to 1 gallon of water). Combine sugar and vinegar and bring to a boil. Add cinnamon and cloves. Drain figs well, and add to boiling syrup. Simmer for 1 hour. Pack hot into jars and cover with syrup. Cover and seal. Makes 7 to 8 pints.

BRANDIED FIGS

2 1/2 cups brandy (apricot or cherry)
2 1/2 cups water
5 lbs. figs
5 cups sugar

Place brandy in a jar, then heat by running hot water on the jar. Wash figs, then puncture each in several places with a fork. Combine sugar and water; cook until sugar dissolves. Add figs. Boil gently for 6 to 10 minutes. Remove figs from syrup and put into hot jars. Boil syrup rapidly for 5 to 8 minutes to thicken the mixture. Pour 1/2 cup of brandy over figs in each jar and fill to within 1/8 inch of top with boiling hot syrup. Cover and seal. Will make about 5 pints.

PEACH JAM
(low-calorie)

2 tsp. unflavored gelatin
3 1/2 lbs. fresh peaches
4 tbsp. liquid sweetener
1 tbsp. cold water
8 tsp. lemon juice

Soften the gelatin in cold water. Peel, pit, and cut peaches into pieces. Place in a kettle without water. Cook over medium heat, stirring often, till peaches are soft. Crush lightly with fork. Measure fruit, add water, if necessary, to make 4 cups of pulp. Add sweetener, lemon juice, and softened gelatin. Return to heat and continue to cook for 1 minute. Remove from heat; ladle into half-pint jars. Each tablespoon measures about 10 calories with 2.5 grams carbohydrate. The same recipe when made with sugar rather than the artificial sweetener is 37 calories per tablespoon. Will make approximately 4 half-pints.

TOMATO AND APPLE BUTTER

2 cups tomato pulp
3 cups sugar
2 cups apple pulp
1 orange

Cook tomatoes and apples till tender and rub through sieve. Measure pulps and combine with sugar and juice and rind of orange. Cook till mixture is thick, stirring frequently. Pour into pint jars; cover and store. Will make approximately 3 jars.

PART IX

Beverages

Whether hot or cold, beverages play an important part in the breakfast menu. However, there is no need for you to start the day with merely a glass of orange juice or a cup of coffee—if you have more creative instincts. Included in this section are thirty-three different and wonderfully tasty drinks to start the morning.

Some of the creamy fruit and milk mixtures are good and nutritious breakfasts-in-a-glass for people in a hurry who still require a sustaining morning pickup.

It is also good to use a blender to make some of these types of beverages, so if you have one, please go ahead and make use of it. A blender makes possible a hundred different morning beverages: frothy, creamy, clear, delicious. And it is a quick way to make the beverage, rather than crushing, creaming, and shaking the fruit and milk ingredients.

Coffee and tea also have many variations, so try a hand with them, too. And speaking of tea, don't forget that many people drink tea here in America, though we seem to always associate that drink with England. As a tea-drinker, I can testify that many hostesses do not take this fact into consideration when serving beverages to a gathering, and it is most unfortunate. So then, always keep tea on hand and inquire about tea-lovers before serving.

Let this section expand your own interests and tastes for breakfast beverages, and see if you can come up with some winners of your very own. Orange juice is fine, but it is not the last word in breakfast drinks.

CRANBERRY JUICE COCKTAIL SUPREME

1 lb. (4 cups) raw cranberries
2/3 cup sugar
4 cups water
cran-cubes for each glass

To make the cran-cubes, pour 1 quart cranberry juice into ice cube trays and set in freezer. Make sure that liquid is thoroughly frozen before using. Four hours should be enough. Remove trays from freezer, take cubes from tray, and use with Cranberry Juice Cocktail Supreme when needed.

To make cocktail, cook berries and water until all skins pop open. Strain through cheesecloth. Heat, add sugar, and then boil for approximately 2 minutes. Chill before serving. Lemon, orange, grapefruit juice, as well as ginger ale combine well with this juice. When serving, place one cran-cube in glass, then fill with cocktail.

EGGNOG LEMONADE COOLER

2 cups warm milk
1/2 cup lemonade (frozen)
1/4 cup instant eggnog
grated peel from 1 lemon

Blend together milk, and eggnog beads in saucepan. Cook over low heat. Add lemonade and stir in well. Pour mixture into glasses and serve garnished with a little lemon peel. Allow approximately as many cups of milk as servings are required.

BREAKFAST EGGNOG

1 1/2 cups frozen orange juice
5 cups milk
2 eggs

Beat eggs with fork until mixture is smooth and creamy. Add thawed orange juice and milk. Stir with vigor and mix well. Chill briefly before serving. Will yield approximately 5 cups.

TIGER LILY

2 cups white grape juice
1 cup orange juice
1/2 cup water
2 cups grapefruit juice
2 tbsp. sugar

Fill glasses half full of shaved ice (using as many glasses as servings are wished, of course) and place each glass in freezer. Combine all ingredients in a large shaker and shake well. Let cool in refrigerator for about 10 or 15 minutes. Take out glasses and juice. Pour. Will serve 5 to 6.

FRUIT MILK PUNCH

1/2 crushed banana
2 tbsp. orange juice
1/4 cup pineapple juice
1 tbsp. lemon juice
pinch of salt
1 cup milk

This is a tasty treat for breakfast. Put all ingredients into a blender and blend at medium speed for several minutes. Cool in the refrigerator for a short time before serving. Makes 2 servings.

STRAWBERRY BREAKFAST GLASS

3 eggs
2 cups sliced strawberries
2 tbsp. sugar
3 cups cold milk

In a mixing bowl or blender mix all ingredients. Blend well. Garnish each serving with a whole strawberry. Will serve 5.

MOLASSES MILK SHAKE

5 cups skim milk
1 small pinch cinnamon
1/2 cup molasses
1 tsp. sugar

Pour milk into large shaker and add molasses. Shake well. Add sugar and cinnamon. Shake again. Chill well before serving. Will serve approximately 6.

CAFE BUTTERSCOTCH

1/2 cup melted butterscotch ice cream
2 tbsp. butterscotch topping
2 cups chilled brewed coffee
2 cups cold milk
2 tbsp. vanilla

Put all ingredients into an electric blender and mix at high speed for about 4 minutes. This length of time will make the mixture foamy. Serve unchilled for a delicious breakfast pick-me-up.

MINT CHOCOLATE DRINK

5 cups milk
2 tbsp. sugar
5 tsp. cocoa
12 candy mint patties

Melt mint patties in double boiler. Mix cocoa and sugar together; add milk. Add mint pattie mixture; cook over low heat. Stir well. Serves approximately 5.

ROOT BEER COFFEE

1 pot coffee
1 small bottle root beer

Make coffee according to desired method (electric or stovetop) and strength. Then add root beer to pot after pouring 1 cup (to allow room for root beer). Stir the brew with a long-handled spoon. Will serve as many as coffee pot capacity will allow.

LEMON BRISK

boiling water
dash of salt
juice of 1 lemon

Bring pan of water to a rolling boil. Add just a pinch of salt. While water is boiling, extract juice from lemon. Pour into saucepan with water, and serve not. A delightful addition to the breakfast scene.

BREAKFAST-STYLE COCOA

1/4 cup cocoa
3 tbsp. sugar
1/8 tsp. salt
peppermint drops (candy)
3 cups milk
1/2 tsp. vanilla
1 cup water

Combine cocoa, sugar, and salt. Add water and cook for 2 minutes over moderate heat, stirring constantly. Add milk and heat only to boiling point. Add vanilla. Remove from heat and serve at once, with 1 peppermint drop candy in each cup. Makes about 6 cups.

BREAKFAST SHAKE

6 cups skim milk
10 tsp. wheat germ
3 bananas

Cut bananas in half and put in electric blender with milk. Run blender at low speed for several minutes until the mixture is smooth and without lumps. Top with added sprinkling of wheat germ and serve in tall glasses. Makes 6 glasses.

MORNING COFFEE MILK SHAKE

5 glasses water
1/3 cup instant coffee
1 tsp. liquid sweetener
4 cups powdered milk
2 tsp. cocoa

Pour water into blender. Add all other ingredients. Cover and blend for 1/2 minute. Chill in the refrigerator for 1 hour and then serve. Makes approximately 5 glasses.

MINTED TEA

2 sprigs mint
1/2 tsp. powdered ginger
1/3 cup hot water
2 cups strong hot tea
1/3 cup orange juice
juice of 2 lemons
1 cup cold water

Soak and roll mint leaves in a bowl or pitcher. Pour in the orange and the lemon juices and hot tea. Stir the ginger into the hot water, then blend with cold water. Add to fruit juice and tea mixture. Chill 1 hour or a bit longer before serving. Serve over ice cubes for a summer breakfast cooler. Makes 3 to 4 tall servings.

MORNING ESPRESSO

4 cups hot (extra strength) espresso coffee
cracked ice
lemon twists
sugar (to taste)

Pour hot strong coffee into tall glasses filled with cracked ice. Serve with lemon twists. Add sugar to individual taste. Makes approximately 4 to 5 glasses. Serve as a perky summer-morning cooler.

ICED SPICED MORNING COFFEE

7 tbsp. instant coffee
2 sticks cinnamon
1/2 cup sugar
10 whole cloves
7 cups hot water

Place coffee, cloves, and cinnamon in a saucepan. Add hot water. Cover and bring just to a boil. Remove from heat and let stand 5 to 8 minutes. Strain to remove the spices. Add sugar and stir until dissolved. Serve over ice cubes. Makes 8 to 10 servings.

RUSSIAN TEA MIXTURE

(This dry mixture is made ahead of the time to be served and combines some very ordinary ingredients for a most extraordinary flavor.)

2 1/2 cups orange-flavored breakfast drink
1 tsp. cinnamon
1/2 tsp. ground cloves
1 1/4 cups sugar
3/4 cup instant tea
dash of salt

Combine the instant orange drink mix, sugar, instant tea, spices, and salt. This mix may be stored in a jar (tightly covered) and will make four cups of the mixture. For each serving of hot tea, place one rounded teaspoonful of the mix in a cup. Add boiling water and stir to dissolve. Serve at once. (For iced tea, dissolve two well-rounded teaspoons of the mix with 3/4 cup boiling water. Pour over ice cubes and serve in tall glasses.)

VERY BERRY COOLER

2 cups sliced strawberries or boysenberries
3/4 cup boiling water
4 cups milk
1/3 cup honey

Pour honey into boiling water and let set. Clean berries well. Place in an electric blender, adding milk. Mix at medium speed until creamy and smooth. Cool water-honey mixtue in refrigerator. When cool, add to the berry mixture. Cool again. Serves approximately 7.

ORANGE-BERRY JUICE COCKTAIL

5 cups strawberries
1/2 cup water
2 1/2 tbsp. sugar
juice of 3 oranges
1 tsp. lemon juice

Rinse strawberries with cold water; remove caps. Into a shallow dish turn the berries. Pour orange juice over them. Let sit for about an hour. Put berries in the blender, along with the orange juice. Mix in the blender for about 1 minute. Add sugar, water, and lemon juice. Mix in blender for about 1 minute. Chill before serving. Makes approximately 4 servings.

CREOLE WARMTH

1 qt. raspberry soda
1 small bottle ginger ale
1 bottle cola beverage

Combine all ingredients in saucepan and heat over low flame or heat. Serve in teacups or coffee mugs. Will serve approximately 8.

COMPANY COFFEE

Mix 1 egg (shell and all) into a pound of coffee. Add 1 cup cold water. Tie coffee in cheesecloth bag large enough to allow room for coffee to swell. Then measure 7 quarts cold water into coffee pot. Immerse coffee bag in water; bring to a boil. Remove pot from heat. Leave bag in water 3 to 4 minutes, or until desired strength is reached. Remove bag and stir. Then serve. Serves 40.

FRUIT BUTTERMILK

1 1/2 cups canned fruit juice
3 tbsp. sugar
3 cups chilled buttermilk

Combine all ingredients and stir to dissolve the sugar. Serve well chilled (will not curdle on standing). Makes 6 servings.

APRICOT-ORANGE TEA

2 1/2 cups apricot nectar
1 cup orange juice
1 cup water
1 tbsp. sugar
1 tsp. ground cinnamon
4 lemon slices
12 whole cloves
2 tsp. instant tea

Combine apricot nectar, orange juice, water, sugar, and cinnamon in a medium-sized saucepan. Insert 3 cloves into each lemon slice; add to saucepan. Heat just to boiling; reduce heat. Cover. Simmer for 5 minutes; stir into tea. Serve hot. Makes 6 servings.

STRAWBERRY TEA

1/2 cup sugar
1/2 cup sliced strawberries
1 can frozen lemonade
2 qts. hot tea

Stir sugar, lemonade, and frozen strawberries into the tea. Serve in large mugs. Will make approximately 10 servings.

COFFEE AUX BANANAS

4 bananas
4 cups strong chilled coffee
1 cup vanilla ice cream
2 cups milk
1 tsp. vanilla

Cut bananas into chunks and combine with coffee, ice cream, milk, and vanilla in an electric blender. Mix at medium speed for approximately 2 minutes or until mixture is thick and smooth. Serve at once. Makes about 7 servings.

PINEAPPLE-ORANGE BREAKFAST-IN-A-GLASS

In a blender, beat together 4 eggs, 1/2 cup crushed pineapple, and 1/3 cup frozen orange juice. Gradually add 4 cups of cold milk. Makes about 6 cups.

PEACH SHAKE SUMMER COOLER

1 large can sliced peaches
1 tsp. mace
4 cups cold milk
2 tsp. nutmeg

In a blender, beat together all ingredients at a low speed, until mixture is creamy and smooth. Cool in refrigerator before pouring. Will make about 6 servings.

SPICED TOMATO COCKTAIL

5 cups tomato juice
dash of pepper
paprika
1/3 cup water
1/2 tsp. onion salt
dash of allspice

Pour tomato juice into large shaker. Gradually pour in water and shake well. Add pepper, onion salt, paprika, and allspice. Shake well. Chill in refrigerator for about 15 minutes before serving. Will serve about 6.

CARROT-LEMON JUICE

1 cup finely ground carrot paste
5 cups frozen lemon juice
1 tbsp. sugar
1/2 cup water

Place all ingredients in a large shaker. (Carrot paste should be made from carrots ground in blender). Shake well. Chill before serving. Will serve 6.

MOCK IRISH COFFEE

1 pot freshly brewed coffee
1/2 tbsp. sugar
5 tbsp. rum extract
1/4 tsp. salt

With long-handled spoon, stir ingredients into coffee pot. Keep heated. Serve very hot in coffee mugs, with a dollop of whipped cream, if desired.

MILK AND HONEY NECTAR

5 cups milk
1 cup honey

Heat milk in saucepan. Keep heat low. When milk is hot, stir in the honey. Stir constantly till honey is dissolved. Serve hot. Will serve 6.

TOMATO HOT

5 cups tomato juice
1/2 tsp. finely chopped onion
pepper and salt

Pour tomato juice into a medium-sized saucepan. Keep heat at a medium level. Pepper and salt well, being sure to use more pepper than salt. Stir in finely chopped onions. Bring to near boil. Serve when hot. Will serve about 5.

PART X

Spreads, Sauces, and Syrups

Here are just a few brief suggestions for luscious toppings and spreads for toasts, pancakes, waffles, coffee cakes, salads, and even eggs. Their use will, of course, be determined by preference, but use them to conjure up other ideas. They are all basic recipes that can be used with substitutes.

These extras in this book add just a pinch of variation and flavor and serve as an incentive to future ideas. Try them on your favorite breakfast foods.

DOROTHY SPREAD

2/3 cup honey
3 tbsp. flaked coconut
1/2 cup peanut butter

With a wooden spoon, mix honey and peanut butter in a small bowl till well blended. Stir in coconut. Use as a spread on plain toast, or bread slices, muffins, or oatmeal (as well as other hot cereals). If desired, make spread without the coconut. Spread generously over bread, sprinkle with coconut and broil until bubbly, and the coconut is golden. Store extra spread in a covered jar in refrigerator. Makes about 1 1/4 cups.

HONEYSCOTCH SAUCE

1/2 cup sugar
1/4 tsp. salt
2/3 cup milk
3/4 cup honey
1/4 cup butter

Combine sugar, honey, salt, butter, and 1/3 cup milk in saucepan. Cook over medium heat, stirring often, till mixture is in soft-ball stage. Stir in remaining milk and cook till sauce is thick and smooth, about 3 minutes. Serve warm over pancakes or waffles. Makes 1 1/2 cups.

ORANGE-CHEESE SAUCE

2 pkgs. cream cheese
1/2 cup fresh orange juice
2 1/2 tsp. sugar
2 tsp. grated orange peel

Allow cream cheese to stand until it reaches room temperature. Beat cheese until it is light and fluffy. Combine orange juice, sugar, and grated orange peel. Add to cheese slowly, while beating. Pour about 2 tablespoons cream cheese sauce over each serving of pancakes. Also, this is good when served over scrambled eggs.

THE CRIMSON TIDE

1/4 cup hot water
1 cup tart red jelly or jam
2 tsp. lemon juice
dash of salt

Add ingredients to water in a very deep bowl. Beat mixture together till smooth. Serve over rolls, fresh fruit, or french toast.

(Combination Toast Spreads)

(The following three recipes are made from ready-made store-bought jellies, jams, etc., and the combinations are really limitless; there are probably a hundred possible combinations. Here however, are three to set the pace. These may seem a bit fancy, but they do make very lovely looking—and tasting—toppings for english muffins, toast, or breakfast biscuits.)

GINGER-GRAPE SMOOTHEE

1 tsp. finely chopped candied ginger
1 cup grape preserves
1/4 cup applesauce

Combine all ingredients. Spread on toast, muffins, cornbread, or biscuits. Makes 1 1/4 cups of spread.

GRAPE JELLY-LADE

1 cup concord grape jelly
1 tbsp. shredded coconut
1/4 cup orange marmalade

Blend all ingredients. Spread on biscuits or on toasted english muffins, along with cream cheese. Makes 1 1/4 cups of spread.

PINEAPPLE GRAPE-NUT SPREAD

1 cup concord grape jam
1/4 cup crushed pineapple, well-drained
1/4 cup chopped macadamia nuts

Combine all ingredients. This is best served with omelets or on fresh hot rolls. Makes 1 1/4 cups.

LEMON MAYONNAISE

Mix 3 tablespoons of lemon juice with 1/2 cup of mayonnaise. Stir well. Serve on toast, muffins, in a breakfast salad, or as a gelatin topping.

LEMON SAUCE

2 egg yolks
2 tbsp. cornstarch
1/8 tsp. salt
3/4 cup sugar
1 cup water
1 lemon, peeled
1/2 rind of lemon

Mix together egg yolks, lemon, and rind with a rotary beater. Run beater at high speed, until the eggs are lemon colored and the rind finely chopped. Add remaining ingredients and blend at high speed with beater till thoroughly mixed. Pour into a saucepan and cook over low heat till thick. Stir constantly. Serve on hot breakfast rolls.

BANANA SAUCE

3 ripe bananas
dash of salt
1 1/2 tbsp. lemon juice
1/3 cup heavy cream
1 cup confectioners' sugar

Put cream into a deep bowl. Peel and break bananas into 1-inch pieces. Add 1 banana to the cream and beat at high speed with rotary beater. Stop beater and add remaining bananas, salt, and lemon juice. Beat again at high speed, slowly adding the sugar 1/4 cup at a time. When the mixture is thoroughly blended, serve at once over oatmeal or fresh fruit.

CARBONATED SYRUPS

For a novel approach to pancake syrups, try adding a 7-oz bottle of lemon-lime carbonated beverage to ordinary syrup. Simmer in saucepan with a half cup of brown sugar for several minutes. Serve immediately. Other carbonated beverages may also be used, with or without the brown sugar, depending upon the type of beverage.

FRUITED SYRUPS

Various types of juices (lemon, orange, apple, berry, prune, pear, etc.) make interesting combinations with ordinary maple base syrup. To mix, merely add one part syrup and one part juice in a shaker. Shake with vigor. Then run hot water over bottle so that when served over waffles, pancakes, breads, etc., syrup will be warm and flavorful.

CHOCOLATE SAUCE

2 squares shredded unsweetened chocolate
1/2 tsp. vanilla
1/2 cup sugar
6 tbsp. hot milk
dash of salt

Heat and melt chocolate in double boiler. Set aside and let cool for brief period (but not long enough to allow chocolate to set and harden again). In a deep bowl, beat together chocolate, sugar, milk, and salt. Stop beating when mixture is creamy and smooth. Serve immediately over waffles, pancakes, or fresh biscuits. Will yield about 3/4 cup.

WHIPPED ORANGE BUTTER FOR PANCAKES

1 cup butter
1/4 cup confectioners' sugar
dash of nutmeg
1/4 cup frozen orange juice

Beat butter till fluffy. Add sugar, nutmeg, orange juice (thawed); continue beating till well blended. Top pancakes with large portions of mixture.

BUTTERSCOTCH SAUCE

1 1/4 cups brown sugar
2/3 cup corn syrup
4 tbsp. butter
3/4 cup light cream

Put sugar, corn syrup, and butter into saucepan. Bring to boiling point; let boil till a little of the mixture, when dropped in cold water, will form a soft ball. Add cream and cool. Serve over pancakes or waffles.

PART XI

Breakfast Extras

Here is where you can really let your imagination in cooking run wild. There are so many wonderful little breakfast "extras" that can be inspired by the ones I have listed in this section.

So you see, you don't have to settle for pancakes, eggs, toast, rolls—even if they are prepared in a special way. Actually, there is no limit to what you can serve for the morning meal. The foods that we set aside as "breakfast only" came about as a matter of tradition. But in all truth, there need be no limit. It's all up to you.

For example: Fritters can be made in just about any flavor—sweet or otherwise. The same is true of doughnuts.

Kabobs are a unique way to spice up an outdoor, patio-style breakfast, and many different fruits, sweets, and meats can be used.

Also included here are appealing little "tasties" for the breakfast table. Add your own ideas and then prepare your own original and enjoyable breakfast.

APPLE-DATE STRUDEL

2 1/2 cups sifted flour
1 tsp. baking powder
butter
1/2 cup pecans
1 pkg. pitted dates
1/4 cup lemon juice
1/2 cup ice water
1/2 tsp. salt
1 egg, beaten
3/4 cup crumbs
1/2 cup sugar
2 lbs. cooking apples
1 tsp. cinnamon

Sift flour, baking powder, and salt together in a bowl. Add egg and 1/4 cup butter, melted. Add 1/2 cup ice water. Stir until blended, then knead to smooth ball on floured surface. Cover with a towel and let sit for about 1/2 hour. Meanwhile, sauté crumbs in butter till light brown. Add nuts and set aside. Peel and core the apples, cut in wedges, then in thin crosswise slices. Mix with remaining ingredients. Roll dough to a long rectangle. Brush with 2 tablespoons butter. Sprinkle with crumb mixture in inner portion of dough. Spread evenly with apple mixture. Then roll from long side, as in jellyroll fashion. Make into the shape of a horseshoe and place (seam down) on a greased baking sheet. Melt 1/4 cup butter and brush some on the strudel. Bake in a preheated 400° oven for about 45 minutes. Serve sliced, hot.

ALMOND BEAR CLAWS

2/3 cup confectioners' sugar
1 egg, slightly beaten
1 can crescent dinner rolls
1/2 cup almond paste
dash of salt
2 tbsp. sliced almonds

Combine sugar, almond paste, 2 tablespoons beaten egg (keep remaining egg for glaze), and salt. Beat till smooth. Unroll dough to form two rectangles. Press to seal dough. Spread the almond mixture down the center. Fold uncovered dough over almond mixture. Cut each strip into 4 pieces. Place on a greased cookie sheet, seam side down. Brush surface with remaining egg mixture. Bake in a 375° oven for about 35–40 minutes, or till done.

PINEAPPLE AND BACON BITS

1 can pineapple rings
1 lb. bacon

Broil bacon to point of near-doneness. Drain pineapple and wrap bacon around small cut pieces. Then fasten with a toothpick, and place in broiler for about 3 minutes. Watch carefully, so that they do not overcook.

APRICOT TURNOVERS

2 1/2 cups sifted flour
3 tsp. baking powder
1/2 cup butter
milk
1/4 cup sugar
1/4 tsp. salt
2 eggs
apricot preserves or jam

In a large mixing bowl, combine flour, sugar, baking powder, salt, and butter. Break eggs into a measuring cup and fill with milk. Add to first mixture and stir to form soft dough. Place on floured surface; knead. Roll into a rectangle. Cut dough into 2-inch squares. Spread the preserves in center of each square and fold to form triangles. Bake on cookie sheet in 425° oven for 12 minutes. Will make about 20.

SWISS-STYLE BREAKFAST

1/2 cup instant oatmeal
1 tbsp. instant dry-milk solid
2 tbsp. chopped almonds
2 tbsp. chopped pitted prunes
1 medium grated apple, unpeeled
1 tbsp. honey
6 oz. apple juice

Combine ingredients and chill for about 10 minutes. Also, this mixture may be prepared in the evening and refrigerated overnight. It can be served with cherries. In the morning, add hot milk or hot water (a small amount) and serve as a cereal. Can be topped with fresh strawberries or other fresh fruit. Will make 2 to 3 servings.

CHERRY DOUGHNUTS

5 cups sifted flour
2 tbsp. baking powder
3 eggs, beaten
3/4 cup milk
1/2 tsp. almond extract
1/4 cup maraschino cherry juice
2 tsp. salt
1/2 tsp. nutmeg
1 cup sugar
3 tbsp. oil
1 jar maraschino cherries
fat for frying

Sift together flour, baking powder, salt, and nutmeg. Blend eggs, sugar, milk, oil, almond extract, cherries, and juice together in another bowl. Gradually add flour mixture. Chill dough if necessary for handling. Turn out onto floured surface and cut with doughnut cutter. Fry in fat till boiling. Drain. Roll or shake warm doughnuts in sugar. Will make three dozen doughnuts.

ORANGE DOUGHNUTS

2 eggs
2 tbsp. soft shortening
grated peel of 1 orange
3 1/2 cups sifted flour
2 tsp. baking powder
1/2 tsp. salt
1 cup sugar
1/2 cup milk
4 tbsp. orange juice
1 tsp. soda
1/4 tsp. cinnamon
fat for frying

Beat eggs and stir in sugar and shortening. Stir in milk, orange peel, and juice. Sift together flour, baking powder, soda, salt, and cinnamon and stir into egg mixture. Turn out onto floured surface and knead for 1 minute. Roll dough out 1/3 inch thick. Let rest for about 20 minutes. Cut with floured doughnut cutter and drop into deep fat, heating to boil. Turn as they rise to surface and show a golden color. Fry for 3 minutes till browned on both sides. Lift from fat and drain on paper towels. Dust with sugar. Makes about 2 dozen.

BREAKFAST POPOVERS

1 cup sifted flour
2 eggs
popover drizzle
1/2 tsp. salt
1 cup milk

Sift together flour and salt into a bowl. Add eggs and milk and beat with beater till smooth. Pour into well-greased heated popover cups, filling about 3/4 full. Bake at 425° for about 40 minutes. Will make about 8 medium-sized popovers. For popover drizzle, cream 1 tablespoon butter with 1/2 cup confectioners' sugar, 1 teaspoon lemon extract, and 1/2 teaspoon water. Use spoon to drizzle over popovers.

PEAR FRITTERS

6 fresh pears
1 cup milk
cooking oil
2 tsp. cinnamon
2 eggs
2 cups pancake flour
1 cup sugar
2 tsp. grated orange peel

Core and slice pears into 1/4- to 1/2-inch rings. Beat egg and milk till well blended. Add pancake mix and stir just till large lumps disappear. Dip pear rings in batter. Fry in deep oil till golden brown. Drain on toweling till crispy. Coat warm fritters with a mixture of sugar, cinnamon, and grated orange peel.

QUICKIE DOUGHNUTS

2 eggs
2 tbsp. butter
3 3/4 cups flour
2 tbsp. baking powder
1/2 tsp. nutmeg
3/4 cup sugar
3/4 cup milk
1 tsp. baking soda
1 tsp. salt

Beat eggs; add sugar and beat in large bowl. Stir in butter, milk, flour, baking powder, baking soda, salt, and nutmeg. Chill dough after mixing well. Roll out 1/3 inch thick and cut with doughnut cutter. Fry in hot grease till golden. Drain. Coat with sugar or frosting.

HONEY BUN ROLL

6 honey-glazed doughnuts
1/2 cup honey
butter

Slice doughnuts in half. Brush insides of doughnuts with butter. Stack them together and pour over 1/2 cup honey. Place on well-greased pan and place in oven at 300° for about 10 minutes. Cool before serving.

CINNAMON ROLLS SALLY

4 cups biscuit mix
1/2 cup sugar
butter
2 cups water
cinnamon-sugar
frosting for rolls

Combine biscuit mix, sugar, butter, and water. Knead dough with hands. Dough should be firm. If not, add a bit more flour or biscuit mix till dough is firm enough to roll out. Take half of dough and roll out on floured surface. Sprinkle with cinnamon-sugar and top with butter. Roll in jelly-roll fashion. Press seam. With a sharp knife, slice pieces about 1/2 inch thick. Repeat this with the other half of the dough. Place all sliced rolls in a deep cake pan, sprinkle with much butter and more sugar with cinnamon. Bake in preheated 350° oven for about 30 minutes. While still hot, drizzle with frosting and serve. Will make about 30 rolls.

Directions for Frosting:

Blend together 1/2 cup confectioners' sugar, 1 tablespoon butter, and 1 teaspoon vanilla. Stir well. Use as a topping for rolls.

BACON ROLL-UP GOODIES

bacon slices
American cheese
india relish

Cut slices of bacon in half; spread with cheese (grated) and relish. Roll up tight and spear with toothpicks. Broil till done. Drain on paper and serve hot with eggs.

CORN STICKS

1 cup sifted flour
3/4 cup cornmeal
2 tsp. baking powder
3/4 tsp. salt
2 tbsp. sugar
1 egg
3/4 cup milk
1/4 cup melted shortening

Heat greased corn-stick pans. Combine all ingredients, beating well with fork, or electric mixer. Pour batter into corn-stick pans. Bake in a preheated 450° oven for about 20 minutes. Will make 8 large corn sticks. Serve with ham or top with cottage cheese for the more weight-conscious.

MARMALADE SLICES

1 loaf french bread
1/2 cup orange marmalade
1/2 cup soft butter
cinnamon

Cut bread into 1-inch crosswise slices. Spread slices with butter, then spread with marmalade. Sprinkle cinnamon over top. Place slices (marmalade side up) on an ungreased baking sheet. Bake in preheated 425° oven for about 5-7 minutes. Will make 8 to 10 slices.

APPLE FRITTERS

1 cup sifted flour
1 1/2 tsp. baking powder
1 cup prepared apple pie filling
1/3 cup milk
frying oil
1/4 tsp. cinnamon
1/4 tsp. salt

Sift dry ingredients into mixing bowl. Beat egg well with fork. Stir mixture into dry ingredients. Add pie filling. Drop batter into hot oil (from a spoon). Fry till fritters are golden brown.

BACON BARS

1/2 cup shredded American cheese
6 slices bacon, crisp and crumbled
2 cups biscuit mix
3 tbsp. bacon drippings

Stir cheese and bacon into dry mix. Make the dough according to package directions for biscuits, substituting bacon drippings for salad oil. Knead as directed for the rolled-type biscuits. Roll out. Cut into 6 10-inch long strips about 1 inch wide. Cut each in thirds, crosswise, to make 18 bars. Place 1 inch apart on an ungreased cookie sheet. Bake at 450° for about 10 minutes. Makes 18 bacon bars.

BANANAS GRECIAN

Fill dessert glasses with sliced bananas. Add pear nectar, covering fruit. Garnish fruit with mandarin orange sections, maraschino cherries, and mint sprigs.

BREAKFAST KABOBS

This recipe need only be as limited as your imagination. Good suggestions are: Rolled-up bacon (fried), sliced bananas, cherries, doughnuts, peach halves, thick ham slices, apple slices, etc. Arrange prettily on a spit, brush with a bit of butter, and cook. These fruits, meats, etc., are a real treat with a serving of scrambled eggs.

CHEESE AND JELLY TURNOVERS

1 can biscuits
2 tbsp. melted butter
1 tsp. cinnamon
strawberry preserves
1/4 cup sugar
1 pkg. cream cheese

Roll each biscuit on a floured surface and form into ovals. Cut cream cheese into 8 slices. Place slice of cream cheese at one end of each biscuit oval. Top with a teaspoon of preserves. Moisten edges with a little water. Fold edge and seal seam. Bake in preheated 425° oven for about 10 minutes, or till golden brown. Brush with butter. Roll in sugar and cinnamon. Serve hot. Will make 8 turnovers.

BANANA AND PINEAPPLE FRITTERS

2 cups sifted flour
1 tbsp. baking powder
1/2 tsp. ground allspice
1/2 cup chopped almonds
2 bananas, peeled and sliced
fat for deep frying
1/3 cup sugar
1 tsp. salt
1 egg, beaten
1 cup milk
1 can pineapple slices
1/2 cup sugar

Sift flour, 1/3 cup sugar, baking powder, salt, and allspice into mixing bowl. Stir in almonds. Blend eggs and milk into mixture. Add liquid to flour mixture, and stir till well blended. Batter should be medium thick. Dip the pineapple slices and banana slices (one at a time) into batter and coat completely. Fry in preheated deep fat till golden brown. Drain on paper toweling. Measure 1/2 cup sugar into paper bag. Add fritters, a few at a time, and shake gently to coat. Serve warm.

Index

3539434

Made in the USA